LOVE, SEX, &
DECEPTION

THE CHRONICLES OF
ONLINE DATING

LISA HULTIN & CLAIRE HULTIN

NEW YORK

LOVE, SEX, & DECEPTION
THE CHRONICLES OF ONLINE DATING
by LISA HULTIN & CLAIRE HULTIN

This copyright is initially represented as a Form TX which is used for dramatic literary works, including fiction, non-fiction, poetry, brochures, reference works, online works, and computer programs. The copyright was formed through Legal Zoom Inc., which has also partnered with VerSign and BBB OnLine. VeriSign is he leading Secure Sockets Layer (SSL) Certificate Authority enabling secure e-commerce and BBB OnLine provides consumer and provider trust regarding resources in business. For more information, address Legal Zoom.com, Inc.

Unless otherwise indications, all quotations, derived concepts, and other data associated with online dating statistics are directly linked to an index and bibliography within the back pages.

Disclaimer: The Publisher and the Author make no representations or warranties with respect to the accuracy or completeness of the contents of this work and specifically disclaim all warranties, including without limitation warranties of fitness for a particular purpose. No warranty may be created or extended by sales or promotional materials. The advice and strategies contained herein may not be suitable for every situation. This work is sold with the understanding that the Publisher is not engaged in rendering legal, accounting, or other professional services. If professional assistance is required, the services of a competent professional person should be sought. Neither the Publisher nor the Author shall be liable for damages arising herefrom. The fact that an organization or website is referred to in this work as a citation and/or a potential source of further information does not mean that the Author or the Publisher endorses the information the organization or website may provide or recommendations it may make. Further, readers should be aware that internet websites listed in this work may have changed or disappeared between when this work was written and when it is read.

ISBN 978-160037-775-4 (paperback)

Library of Congress Number 2010925450

Published by:

MORGAN JAMES PUBLISHING
1225 Franklin Ave. Ste 325
Garden City, NY 11530-1693
Toll Free 800-485-4943
www.MorganJamesPublishing.com

Cover Design by:
Rachel Lopez
Rachel@r2cdesign.com

Interior Design by:
Bonnie Bushman
bbushman@bresnan.net

In an effort to support local communities, raise awareness and funds, Morgan James Publishing donates one percent of all book sales for the life of each book to Habitat for Humanity.
Get involved today, visit
www.HelpHabitatForHumanity.org.

For Claire, my incredibly supportive daughter, who on occasion reversed roles for her single mom.

To my wonderful mother, Lisa, who lent her ears, knowledge, and has been there through my dilemmas in dating, relationships, and even online dating.

Last, but not least, to all the fearless men and women who take a chance online hoping to find genuine true love.

CƷ℥Ɔ

ACKNOWLEDGEMENT

First and foremost, we want to show great appreciation and are forever indebted to all the people who have participated and shared their countless stories about their online dating experiences. We want to thank psychologist Colleen Long for collaborating with us on insider tips and commentary sprinkled throughout the book. She trained for ten years in clinical psychology and uses both her education as well as "field research" (Date Doctor Diaries http://datedoctor.onsugar.com) in the City of Los Angeles to help her clients find the love of their life. She additionally runs psychotherapy groups for Love And Relationship Addiction (L.A.R.A.) addressing patterns of seeking unhealthy or toxic relationships. We also want to thank Stewart Johnson and Udara Soysa for their excellent team work in helping us build our website, and blog, www.LoveSexandDeception.com.

Furthermore, we also want to acknowledge Autumn Conley for her tremendous effort in editing our book as well as acknowledge her distinctive talent with the many books she has edited thus far. We would also like to express our deepest gratitude to the talented and innovational photographer Richie Arpino for creating a unique piece of art and photography as the cover of Love, Sex, and Deception: The Chronicles of Online Dating. His work in Atlanta and at http://www.arpinosalon.com/ regarding his fabulous and innovational photography makes an incredible statement. Special thanks to Meagan McBrayer and John O'Hara for being the exemplary models for the book cover and also Rameda Green for being an excellent make-up artist for the shoot. We want to thank Christie Moore for her fantastic graphic design work for the cover. Finally, we would also like to thank all the people out there who have made an effort into bringing the meaning of this book to life.

CONTENTS

CONTENTS

INTRODUCTION

We are a mother and daughter that have dated online, compared notes, collected hundreds of hilarious dating stories from around the country, and decided to write a trendy little lit concerning research, short stories, tips, and tricks that are related to personal internet dating experiences. Part of the impetus for doing the book-and the rational for the title: Love, Sex, and Deception: The Chronicles of Online Dating is that throughout online dating, everyone has either experienced finding true love, to great sex, or has at least been deceived once or twice.

The truth is we have all roamed through bookstores, surreptitiously searching shelves for a book to help guide us through a perplexing time known as "dating limbo." All we wanted was something we could relate to while enduring the single life, especially the cyber world of online dating. Everyone enjoys a "comfort book" that guides us and makes our questions and desires feel less foreign.

Thus, we have captured countless online dating stories from real people, whether it is full of satire, comedy, or just plain touching and exhilarating. Throughout our research of people's real experiences, we have been able to provide a book that not only is an entertaining read but a guide of tips and tricks to help you along the way. Stay optimistic and on the bright side! If your lovely date's toupee' somehow blows off flipping cartwheels down the tarmac while you board the plane to the tropics, order two scotches and start drinking early. Remember Cosmo once voted Telly Salavas "sexiest man alive!" Endure my friend because 12 percent of online meetings are resulting in marriage.

We undergo the struggles of perplexing transitions, yet we still strive for love and romance. Whether we find the right relationship, get married, or just find friends through the dating network, we are traveling down a path with many interesting stories to tell. One of the reasons that we have taken the time to interview and research the real life situations of online dating is to be able to share amongst others that they are not alone. There is irony in the pursuit of love as you will read, even if you are 90 and only get to experience it briefly. It rivals nirvana and while it doesn't happen often, it is still worth tremendous effort. Look on the bright side and stay optimistic. Everyone deserves to be in a great relationship. Enjoy reading not only a fun book, but learn what to watch out for and how to make the most of online dating.

We would still love to hear from many other men and women who have similar stories that they would like to share with us. If you have a story that you'd like to share, send them to our email address at lisaandclaire@hotmail.com. If you enclose your name and a good story, we'll do our best to get back to you and put you on our newsletter mailing list.

Please visit our website at www.LoveSexandDeception.com and good luck!

CHAPTER 1

A NEW FRONTIER

*"I once sent my picture to a Lonely Hearts Club, and they
sent it back saying, "Thanks, but we are not that lonely."*

—Bob Hope

Never in my wildest dreams did I imagine being single
in my forties hoping for a second chance at love, or have a
daughter looking for a first chance at love—both of us online
and dating! "What... forgo the territory of technology to find a
good man... never!"

—Lisa

These days almost everyone knows at least one couple who
met online, fell in love, and tied the knot. With one click of the
mouse, you can literally peek out of your window to see that
the globe has shrunk into your backyard, erasing geographical
borders and cultural barriers. Perhaps the appeal is the exotic
or magical quality of a potential cyber-romance, nurtured in
the privacy of your own home or office as you search for a
prospect. After all, where else can you quickly, safely, relatively,

and anonymously find someone that matches your wish list? Certainly not in a bar!

At the advent of Internet dating, the person searching for a partner through online dating was perceived as lonely, desperate, and socially inept. "What's the matter? Can't you find a date?" was the sentiment echoed by many. With the explosion of Internet usage, that image has changed altogether, as evidenced by more than 800 dating sites and sixty million subscribers.

"Goodbye, stigma... hello, gorgeous!" is the new attitude these days about online dating, as hundreds of thousands of busy professionals with little spare time flock to the websites to find that special someone. If you are unattached and are not online, you are considered a social dinosaur. The traditional way of meeting someone at weddings, work, church, bars, through friends, or in the aisle of a grocery store is no longer the means to an end in the twenty-first century.

Believe it or not, personal ads date back some 300 years to the matrimonial agencies of the eighteenth century, when lonely bachelors would publicize that they were hoping to recruit a wife. In that era, being over twenty-one and single was considered a bit weird. In the 1990s, personal ads started to become acceptable due to the widespread popularity of the Internet. Match.com launched a dating website that turned romance and courtship on its head! It has now become a billion-dollar business with thirty websites in eighteen languages and more than fifteen million subscribers—truly a modern-day phenomenon now in the mainstream. The competition is growing every day with new sites offering mobile connections and specialized categories from vegetarians to seniors, from cheating wives to women behind bars. Yes, sexy prisoners but no conjugal visits. From homosexuals to heterosexuals and even mad scientists who want to test your DNA to find the "Perfect Match," they are all out there, online and looking.

So why not give it a try? If traditional blind dates aren't bringing Cupid into the picture and 12 percent of all online meetings result in marriage, why not log in? You could get lucky—and at the very least, you will meet some interesting people. However, proceed with caution. If you linger in cyber space long enough searching for love, the chances are you will find one of three things: *LOVE, SEX, OR DECEPTION*, as seen through the many experiences of these people. Learning more about the opposite sex sometimes happens just by listening to their stories. Reality is the best education!

INTERNET SERIAL KILLER OR HUSBAND MATERIAL?

Yes, there is hope after forty! A conversation with a genius P.R. maven at Red Branch Public Relations turned to the subject, as it often does, of finding men in New York. She was convinced that once you are "over the hill," it is virtually impossible. Well, I said, "I met my husband on the internet when I was in my forties."

After a dead silence on the other end of the phone, Sabina said, "You're kidding! THAT gorgeous man?"

A dozen years ago, I was home recovering from surgery, bored with daytime TV, and I decided to surf the net for personals. On one of the dating sites, I saw a picture of a man that was very appealing, sort of resembling Mr. Big in *Sex and the City*. His profile had the top ten things he was looking for in a woman (something he got a lot of grief about) and a bonus question... you had to like France and the French. Well, I had attended the Chamber Syndicate de la Haute Couture and lived in Paris for a year after college, so that was easy. The rest were along the lines of being smart, politically aware, loving sex, and being tall. My tall answer was perfect. "I'm 5'4", but always in sexy three-inch heels, and I LOVE tall men."

We emailed each other for about a month, and one day he emailed, "My friends think I am working too hard and turning into a bore. Do you have any advice?"

I typed back, "Why don't you take a good looking blonde out and buy her a drink?"

We met the next week and hit if off. I would have invited him back to my place, but my brother was convinced he was an Internet serial killer, so that waited for the next date.

There were lots of dates, and we eventually fell for each other and decided to get married. He popped the question, and I said yes, with only one stipulation. The wedding had to be a surprise, because I did not want my mother to know. She formerly was the fact checker at the *The New Yorker*, and her obsession over the details would drive me crazy. I always hosted Thanksgiving, so we decided to get married that next afternoon, inviting family and friends to leftovers. That afternoon, as everyone meandered around nibbling on sandwiches in their house slippers, the doorbell rang, and in stepped a Justice of the Peace. In my cashmere sweater and skirt, I announced, "I know you thought we might be getting engaged, but Frank and I are now getting married." Supposedly, the look on my father's face was amazing, which I totally missed. My mother was thrilled, and as it turned out, grateful to enjoy the moment. We had champagne, a surprise wedding cake pulled out of the closet, and a lot of surprised, happy faces. We eventually slipped out to dinner to celebrate at Beckman Tavern in Rhinebeck. We have been happily married for eleven years and always enjoy celebrating our anniversary the day after Thanksgiving.

Anne in Manhattan New York

This is a great example of the power of initiative and being proactive. Many of us sit around waiting for the other one to make the first move. Anne actually stepped outside of the comfort zone and encouraged him to take her out. Sometimes, just because you're the woman—doesn't mean you have to act like a girl. Why not be a little assertive. Men think it's sexy!

JAZZ AND CARNAL MOONLIGHTING

As for online dating, first dates are a lot like the tagline from the great TV show *Wide World of Sports*—"the thrill of victory and the agony of defeat." With online dating, victory isn't as easily defined, as crossing the finish line first... it's more complicated. Your date has to look vaguely like her picture, must arrive at least somewhat on time, should remember your first name, and must speak a language you both can understand.

I thought this first date, my seventeenth date of 2009, could be a winner. We had lots in common: grown children, similar backgrounds, jobs, hobbies, and a love for jazz. It didn't require long telephone conversations to convince her to meet me for dinner. My offer is always the same, "You pick the restaurant, and I'll pick up the tab." There are great advantages to meeting at a restaurant. The lights are dim so you both look better. You worry less because alcohol is readily available, and you quickly learn if she is confused by more than four pieces of silverware.

She insisted on meeting at a very obscure, off-the-beaten-path little sushi restaurant in the 'burbs'. I got to the restaurant first, and when she walked in, conversation stopped and heads turned. Linda was a classic southern beauty with auburn hair, piercing blue eyes, and long tan legs in a pair of nosebleed Jimmy Choos. Her jewelry was serious too: a diamond ring that spanned from one knuckle to another. To put it bluntly, she was HOT!

She said she wanted to sit in the back, and the hostess obliged us. We were either going to hit it off, or she was hiding from embarrassment. If conversation was bait, then I was reeled in from her attention to detail and accurate memory of my profile. As we are leaving the restaurant, she told me that she had a great CD of Miles Davis, the jazz legend. "Why don't you listen to a few tracks with me in my car? It's the white Mercedes E-500," she said. A $125,000 car? Clearly, she did well in her divorce settlement.

When we arrived at her car, she said, "Let's sit in the back seat. The stereo is incredible from there." My night was getting a lot better and fast! Jazz and a beautiful woman in the back seat of a car? Oh, twist my arm!

She clicked the remote, and the 480-horse power screamed to life. I hopped into the back. "Darling, can you help me get these heels off?" she asked. The paparazzi couldn't have gotten a better shot! As I peeled off her sexy stilettos, I couldn't help devouring her long, tan legs with my eyes, and at the top of them—NOTHING! I mean, she had an incredible mind, but no panties. What a beautiful sight!

The windows were thoroughly fogged. *Now we are getting somewhere,* I said to myself. *First base...second base...third... and I'll be sliding into home plate! What the hell, I'm out? Who the hell is that?* Suddenly, someone was rapping on the window with a large flashlight. My date reached over and slowly lowered the window without a word. In the front of my now open window was a VERY LARGE MAN with a badge and a holstered gun, shining a flashlight in my face. I am a COO, so I immediately cringed at not being able to complete that successful merger we WERE about to execute before we were so rudely interrupted. NOW, I was facing a cop with my pants pulled down to my ankles, and it was not a beautiful sight!

He looked at my license for a second and pointed the flashlight of truth at my date. "Linda, I thought we talked about this kind of behavior."

I kept thinking to myself, *Uhh, her name is Linda... no need for her ID?... uh... no vanity plate...I'm f—*!*

The officer looked at me dead straight in the eye and said, "Sir, are you aware this woman is MARRIED to a judge?"

I answered, "NO. I had no clue she was married." *Hell, this can't get any worse,* I thought. The agony of defeat, and it was going to land me right in the local jail cell.

The officer gently nodded his head. "Sir, I think it is time you get out of my BROTHER'S car and go home!" And that is exactly what I did—albeit within the speed limit for all forty-two miles.

Married women who make out in their husbands' cars: a revelation and activity that I won't ever forget! I finally made it home, kissed my granite driveway, and checked to see that everything was supposed to be attached was attached. I think I need a BREAK from online dating...well, for a while at least.

Mike in Atlanta, Georgia

Ahhh the old adage—"if it's too good to be true, it usually is," comes to mind here. Mike fell victim to the fantasy. He saw this beautiful woman, sparkling conversation (and apparently sparkling fingers) and fell right into her trap. This story underscores the importance of waiting until you know someone before running the bases. What if this woman was an IV drug user? What if she carried venereal diseases? All of these scenarios are likely with someone that exhibits such impulsive behavior. Unfortunately, we no longer live in the era of free love. We have AIDS, Gonorrhea, HPV and other incurable STD's that can turn one night of passion into a lifetime of pain.

SILENT MALBORO MAN

I met a wonderful man online who was tall, gray, and handsome! He fit my *modus operandi* and was definitely my forte. Our very first date, we decided to meet at a nice Thai restaurant in mid-town Atlanta. He was an absolutely beautiful specimen of masculinity with broad shoulders, a John Wayne swagger, and rugged good looks. Although he was a quiet man of few words, conversing with him was like pulling nails out of plywood at best. I upheld most of the conversation that evening with his random few interjections, but I was nonetheless mesmerized! This man was a successful developer with social status who owned his own plane, which he flew himself. WOW! He could have been a deaf mute; I would have eagerly learned sign language. He oozed confidence and ultimately managed to switch the light on my libido. Confidence is such a turn-on! We all know the rules about kissing on the first date, but screw that! I could not WAIT for a long, hot, tongue-wrestling kiss. "Let's skip dessert. Check, please," I said as I motioned to the waitress. I kissed him goodnight for an enticing first date!

Our next date was a wild game party at his home complete with his staff cooking and serving wild boar, quail, and elk coupled with all the southern sides. His house was a bona fide panty trap, totally gorgeous and stately. I was ecstatic that he had included me to meet his friends. Was this an omen that I was maybe special, or just another shot in the dark from a great hunter? I had not a clue. I barely saw him, although he did introduce me to some fraternity brothers. Mostly, he was just busy. Eventually, all the guests left, and he turned and took my tiny little hand in his and started to half drag me up the stairs to his bed without one spoken word.

"Sweetie, it's so late... let's just cuddle on the sofa for a bit. I really do have to get home to my kids," I whispered softly in his ear. I wasn't about to be bagged and mounted without more effort on his part—at least some flowers. I have to admit his skin smelled so delicious! As we were kissing on his worn leather sofa, I opened my eyes to a multitude of dead animals, stuffed and hanging on the walls. A huge moose head was glaring at my every move. *Was that his last girlfriend?* I wondered. To top it off, his bird dogs jumped all over me, panting profusely, leaving a trail of saliva and dog hair all over my dress. Christ resurrected could not salvage the annihilation of the mood.

So, the third date is a charm, right? Or is it three strikes, you're out? What is it about the three-date thing with men? Something about a return on some kind of investment. Who can figure their reasoning, and what does money have to do with it? I was turning forty, which was depressing, but hey, it's the new thirty, and I was keeping it all together. He took me out for my birthday, and we wined and dined at a cozy little restaurant. The food was divine! I was so stuffed and drunk I was worried sick I would either fart or belch before the evening was over. Again, there were no deep conversations—just a few caveman responses here and there. I sized him up as rich, handsome, masculine, and confident, so who cared if he could carry on a conversation! I was beginning to like it quiet! It was a commendable dinner, and I invited him in for a nightcap—his favorite, bourbon on ice.

I lit a candle, popped in a CD of soft music for a little "le mood" atmosphere, and noticed he was gulping down his bourbon like ice water. He embraced me with his strong, burly arms and laid me back on the sofa, passionately kissing me. Within a heartbeat, he unlatched my bra with one hand and managed to de-shirt me with the other, burying his face in my 36 DDs, declining to come up for air. Where do men learn these tricks? Is there a class somewhere? It was a most inopportune time for the CD to skip, but skip annoyingly it did. Embarrassed, I raced over topless to change it to the next song, and when I turned around, my jaw fell to the floor. My date was totally naked on my sofa wearing nothing but a huge grin. He had beautiful teeth! Had he incurred a lack of oxygen in the brain? He was laying there speechless striking the "COME AND GET ME" pose. I had no idea where to look in between the flickering light. *Oh my God! What is that!* I thought.

Straining my eyes, I could see what looked like a huge oversized robust baton. The closer I got, the more it resembled a tall light house beckoning for it's vessel to port. As attracted physically as I was to him, I just wasn't emotionally there yet. I mean, does a little boob action signal to a man that it's time to move directly past go and collect at the bank? Something told me that the naked sofa trick had worked for him before. I sat down with a doe-in-the-headlight look and said, "Sugar, I'm sorry, but I'm not going to take my pants off." The screeching sound of brakes and deafening silence was altogether too much. My date was going south, and the lighthouse had shrunk to a stub.

"What about birthday sex?" he uttered with a baffled look.

"It is my birthday, but I am not going to have sex with you at this time," I exclaimed.

With a sad face and a tone he quipped, "Well, I just better go home then," as he pulled up his pants, commando style.

I could sense a huge rejection, and I hated to send him home empty handed. On the way to the door, I swung by the freezer and grabbed a big frozen tupperware of spaghetti sauce I had made earlier. "Here, darling, sit this on your lap as you drive home and enjoy," I said as I closed the door.

He did call a few days later but never mentioned or apologized for his presumptuous behavior. However, he did rave about my sauce. There was never a fourth date. Patience is a virtue, and obviously he had none.

Lisa in Atlanta, Georgia

Blame it on the saying "third time is a charm," or maybe it is the other women who are more than eager to prostitute themselves out, all for a candlelit dinner and one too many vodka tonics—but this man's behavior would not have been there had it not worked before. At some point, one woman must have reinforced this Pavlovian prince. Lisa did well to send him packing with his pasta sauce. A man that truly respects a woman and wants something more substantial than a romp in the hay would have made that fourth date. Unfortunately for her, she had to learn this lesson on her birthday. Unfortunately for him, he was the only one in the birthday suit.

VEGAS MR. BREAST MAN

Online dating is an exciting smorgasbord of possibilities. I am convinced that much of America is a spin-off indirectly… a minimum of 50 percent of a replay of *Jerry Springer*. When someone says to me, "You wouldn't believe my online dating experience!" my response is "I'll believe anything." This comes after 300 dates and thousands of courting dollars. "YES, I would believe that any friggin thing you could possibly dream up can and does happen, especially if the women are in their late thirties to early fifties." So, women throw out those consulting books of how to trap your man, and just be yourself. When the chemistry is right, ignore the rules.

I have a 3,000-mile search from my home in Las Vegas, so anyone could pop up on the screen, as did this beautiful blonde in a sheer burgundy tube top from Ft. Lauderdale, Florida. She looked like Christie Brinkley with a great face, lips, smile, and curves to pull me into pure hot bliss! She must have been firm under the muscle with easily a 34 DD, size 2-4 waste and bottom. I thought to myself, *Hey, you know when you're on the surface; it's worth grabbing, right?* She appeared to be a gorgeous handful! Her skin looked supple, and the package looked too good to be true with her sweetness dominating her smile—a little precious smile. Yes, there was finally someone to make into a Cinderella. Beautiful teeth have always been a thing for me. Once I was with a woman and her teeth came out and this dog couldn't hunt.

Cindy, my possible Cinderella, wouldn't respond to my repetitive emails, so finally I wrote: "I know you don't know me, but if you give me a chance and just talk to me, I promise I will change your life! You will experience the passion to become Cinderella... for the rest of your life! I promise you... your life will change forever. 100 percent guaranteed."

My persistence paid off. She responded, and we gradually started talking on the phone. I could sense that she was the little sweet simple schoolteacher. She never probed about my assets or if I belonged to a country club or how much money I made. She seemed interested in just me. I said, "Cindy, I want to fly you to Vegas next weekend."

"Oh, no! I couldn't do that. What would my family and friends think?"

I thought, *who really gives a s—*? *My goodness, you're forty-six years old and have been divorced three times, and you are worried about a bunch of s—* *from the Howdy Doody cheering section!*

"I'm from the south (in truth, a transplant from Cleveland) and I just don't know you well enough yet," she exclaimed. She went on to say, "Well, this is way too soon for me, to know you! That is moving too fast. You seem a little aggressive and way too pushy."

I hated to hear that, and it is something men hear all the time. I mean, how much time is there in life for all of us at this age? We could be dead tomorrow!

Her response was, "Well, I would love for you to come visit me next month."

On a Wednesday, I told her, "I will be there in two days—this Friday," and I made reservations for the entire weekend.

She was everything and better than I expected. I took her shopping and bought her a sexy little cocktail dress. I love to spoil women, and she really appreciated the attention. We wined and dined and danced the weekend away, and we almost it seems went on a dry humping spree everywhere from the parking meter into the nightclub. We were having a blast getting to know each other. Of course, she told me "No!" often, but a moment later, she would be letting me feel her up under her shirt. GOD, she did have inch-long erasers—something her girlfriend told me before over the phone. They were so firm, so soft, and so gorgeous. Her legs and bottom looked like a twenty-year-old's, even though she was in her early forties.

At one point during the weekend, she said, "John, I don't know anyone as outrageous, passionate, attentive, and extremely aggressive as you. You're a really bad boy! You said that you would sweep me off my feet, and you are getting there, but stop trying to spread my legs because this is our first date! THIS IS OUR FIRST DATE!"

Again, my response was, "WHO REALLY GIVES A S—*? I just flew 2,500 miles to get a little loving from a classy hot woman." I promised her it was only the beginning.

She wouldn't sleep with me, and I stayed in a hotel, but I know that more often than naught, those goody little two-shoes are tigers in bed once they fall in love with you. "Baby, I'm flying you to Vegas next weekend," I told her before I left that weekend.

"I would love to visit you, John, but I have to have my own room," she insisted.

I said, "Honey, we have spent so much time together and talked so much that it's like we have been on fifty dates!" I will admit that I got a little grouchy about that, but okay, I get it. I would be patient for this one. I flew her in the next weekend and took her to the Wynn Hotel. We went to Trist, danced, and drank pomegranate martinis. Then, I took her to New York, New York to see Chris and Joey, the best two dueling piano players in Vegas!

The minute we walked in, they said, "John, you're here! Who'd you bring this time? Oh, another hot one. *Oh, God, guys did you have to say that?* I thought.

We had a crazy time, and when we went back to my room, we started fooling around a bit. It started getting heavy while we were making out, so I started kissing her more, and she said, "Are you tired?"

That was it! I was finally going to love this woman with all my heart! I said, "Yes, I'm tired. Let's go to bed."

She said, "Yeah, good idea. I am beat." She got up, kissed me, and said, "It is awesome being with you!" Then she went straight to the guest room, closed, and locked the door. I couldn't believe it! She locked the sucker! I mean, here she was, all over me in that hot, sexy little dress with her bulging cleavage, supposedly in the sexual peak of her forties. What the crap happened?

The next morning, I took her to the airport, still crazy about her. When she got home, she gave me a call, and broke off the relationship. I was devastated—well, for a few minutes, anyway. "Why are you ending this, Cindy?" I asked over the phone.

"You lied to me, John, and I'm very upset," she said. "The girls got on the computer after I told them your last name and checked you out! You are ten years older than you say you are!" she asserted.

I answered, "I never lied! My staff did that. I told you. Honey, they do everything for me but my profile, which I wrote. They wouldn't change it when I caught the error because they said if I didn't put down that I was under fifty, it would cut my hits down by 75 percent, which would hurt."

"Once a liar, always a liar. I can never trust you," she said.

"What difference does it make? You love my butt, so when I turn sixty, just take off ten years, because I look it!" I exclaimed.

"You do look great for your age," she said.

I said, "Thanks, honey," but she wouldn't take me back. We were supposed to go on a Caribbean trip.

All I can say is that she had a great set of boobs and now I'm back looking for a new pair.

John in Las Vegas, Nevada

> *This is a classic example of an online introduction that is eventually demystified. Age is the most common lie online. There is nothing more flattering than looking younger than your age, but a little or big white lie can call into question someone's character. Is manipulating the numbers worth a potential relationship or in his case worth the chance of coming back to bite you in the____? Honesty is the best policy!*

AN EVENING WITH A MACHINE GUN

Frank is an IT guy at a big company. It would be unfair to compare him to Rick Moranis, because he is better looking than that, so do me the favor of imagining an older, slightly taller, more attractive version of him in his *Honey, I Shrunk the Kids* era. We connected through Craigslist and were on our first date.

I had to promise to just go along with whatever plans he had in store for us for the evening, and he would not tell me what those plans were until we pulled into the parking lot of each activity for the evening. "Or we can just go to Starbucks and talk, and it will suck. Bring your passport, closed-toe shoes, and a full tank of gas" was all the information I received.

We drove an hour to Manchester and got off at the airport exit. "Can you fly a plane?" Frank asked.

"Um, no."

"Neither can I, so I guess we won't be doing that."

So instead, we visited a firing range. There, I was handed a semi-automatic machine gun. At first I protested, "I'm not comfortable with this." I whimpered as the clerk had me sign a form swearing that I was not a felon, had consumed no alcohol, and was not mentally ill. We shot rounds for about an hour. We were not the only couple there, which says a lot about Manchester, New Hampshire on a Friday night. As we were leaving the firing range he looked me up and down and told me I was not dressed appropriately for our next stop and needed something dressier than the jeans and T-shirt I was wearing. Fortunately I was returning from a business trip and had a suitcase in the back. Surely, I was the only woman at the firing range restroom changing into a dress that evening.

Then we went out for dinner at a high-end restaurant where he ordered everything for us both—including the tequila, which was the only type of alcohol we consumed for the evening. Now you modern ladies reading this may bristle at the thought of someone presuming to order your food, but after years of boorish, ungentlemanly behavior, it was pretty heady to meet someone with this sort of old-fashioned charm coupled with his slight Texan drawl (yes, Frank was from Texas, as if the machine gun wasn't a giveaway). We got back in the car for an hour's drive to Hampton Beach.

A moonlit walk in the sand along the water followed with the bright lights and noise of the honky-tonk strip in the background. "Time for the ballet," he said as we headed back to the car. Since it was ten p.m., I was wondering if we were boarding a flight for Russia for a show, but that was not the case.

Over the state border into Massachusetts, we pulled up to what is commonly referred to as a gentlemen's club, or as I prefer to call it, a strip joint. *In for a dime, in for a dollar,* I thought to myself. *Why not?* So, in we went. Think of a high-end version of the Bada Bing from *The Sopranos*. The many attractive young ladies really weren't doing what I would call dancing, but the guys around their stage didn't seem to mind. Other gals circled the stage selling Jell-o shots. I'm glad I didn't buy one because apparently, it included a rather lascivious exposure of the server's breasts as she handed you the shot.

Frank asked one of the passing vixens for Tracy. Tracy is a licensed massage therapist who also takes part in the circus scene around the stage, giving back massages. So yes, I got a chair massage at a strip joint. There was nothing improper about it other than the naked women rolling around on the stage twenty-five feet away from our table. Frank gamely offered to call over one of the dancers for a table dance, but at this point, it was one a.m., and I had a 100-mile drive home to contend with. Plus, our table seemed a little rickety. "They don't really dance on the table," Frank advised.

I never did get to find out exactly how the table dance worked, thankfully. Instead, we took off in the Subaru, dropped him off at his car, and I drove back home by two thirty a.m. "Do one thing every day that scares you," warned Eleanor Roosevelt. Thanks to Frank, I have banked about a week's worth of doing so after that night. I woke up the morning after the 'best date ever' to find this email waiting for me: "If I had to guess, based on the condition you're in this morning, I'd say you had a hell of a date. Walking through the front door at three a.m. and smelling like gunfire, cologne, massage oil, and tequila, with sand in your shoes and stripper glitter in your hair—seriously, how did you manage that?"

Kathy in Madison, New Hampshire

Wow! This is what I call a "whirlwind of a date." Apparently this A type is a meticulous planner and chances are you may never get bored. Adventurous types that like excitement and change of environment are often a great match. I wouldn't be surprised if one day you find that engagement ring in one of those jello shots made especially just for you.

From Barcelona To San Francisco

It had been two and a half years since my husband died suddenly of a heart attack. I was left a widow at age forty-five with four sons, two of them still in high school. As an ex-patriot American living in Europe, I hoped to stay there until my last son finished high school. This was the early 1990s, and to keep in touch with my American culture, I spent a lot of time on the Internet in chat rooms with other grieving widows and people of like-minded faith.

Mark, a very recent widower from the U.S. west coast, dropped into the chat room one evening. Instant messaging turned into "get-acquainted emails," which soon turned into rather expensive transatlantic phone calls. As the manager of a manufacturing firm, Mark was able to visit Europe on business and arranged a visit to my home. Our first date in person was after three months of chatting online. We explored downtown Madrid and visited many cafés and bars, enjoying fried squid and *café con leche*.

It didn't take long for us to realize that we wanted to get married. This involved my packing up and leaving Spain after twenty-two years, blending two families together for a total of six sons! Our wedding day was one of sweet sorrow. My sons were grieving because they were leaving their home and friends to move to a new culture halfway across the world. It was also hard for them to embrace another man as a father figure. However, within a short time, the stepbrothers became fast friends, and they adjusted well to our new situation.

It has been twelve years since Mark and I met and got married, and what we both realized along the way is that life is short. Unexpected things can happen which we cannot control, but we can enjoy each day that God has given us. We are still very much in love and have now lived in China for six years, and share twelve grandchildren.

Marilyn in San Francisco, California

This is such a great example of how the world really can become one's oyster through the Internet. No longer are we bound by the confines of our hometown, our family's directive, or our alma mater. We can chat with someone on the other side of the earth! I think this story really is a fantastic demonstration of the power of the Internet and how, if used in the right way, can become a connector to people from all walks of life.

CHAPTER 2

SEXUALITY ONLINE.
A PRIORITY BETWEEN
THE SEXES

Is there any talent? Talent is a synonym for chemistry, which likely creates the potential for a great relationship where someone eventually may pop the question. A woman in *lust* wants her partner to give her a box of chocolates. A woman in *love* wants her partner to give her a diamond. A man, on the other hand, wants one thing, regardless of whether he is in lust or in love—and that one thing is sex. Let's establish that it takes up quite a bit of space on the right side of his brain. The online menu is very visual and often the component of initial interest or reaction of a prospect. The reality is that sex is a prevalent activity in the complex maze of abundant choices in online dating. There is a lot of "hooking up," which for some is a sport and for others a gamble for a potential relationship. If you are inclined in this direction there are signs to tell if they might be good in bed. There is nothing worse than bad sex, particularly when it is followed by "I'll call you," which has about as much chance of happening as a blizzard in the Sahara.

Being good in the sack is a gift few are born with, and great sex has the power to smooth over a set of ruffled feathers. It is a skill, a talent, and like many skills and talents, you either have it or you don't. You can learn to master the skills involved, but an unfortunate few just never quite learn or pick up the skills at all. If you are meeting someone look closely when their clothes are on, you will know then and there if you have any interest in taking them off. Attraction, sometimes a mystery to define, is absolutely the key ingredient; however, looks have nothing to do with sexual prowess. If you have ever fallen for a stunning face only to find that magnetism below the belt was tepid at best, you know this to be true. Some beautiful people are just plain frigid, and no amount of coaxing can unleash their inhibitions or ignite their passions. I have seen it prescribed by both gynecologists and ministers that a little alcohol can be quite the aide in loosening one's expressive vulnerability. This may be true, but the one thing guaranteed to keep the sheets ablaze is confidence in your ability to be vulnerable with your partner. Men with talent have a certain body language that is affectionate and warm mannerisms in conversation with women. Attentiveness is such a seducing quality!

Ladies, shake it up! Keep an open body language at the hips when on the prowl. I know it sounds Neanderthalish but it's just that obvious, One study in Belgium revealed that a sexologist could guess a woman's orgasmic ability 80 percent of the time just by the way she walked! If her hips are loose and her stride is long, her sexual energy is good, and the Os will keep on coming—a tune men will hit and repeat as often as possible. Men love it when women are playful and flirty. Send him a flirty text letting him know he is on your mind. The strut says a lot. People who like being in their bodies will want to be in yours. If someone is comfy in their own skin and relaxed, chances are that is how they will be in bed. Women who take small steps and keep their arms and legs crossed tightly all the time are not going to just open up overnight. It is the same for guys who close their bodies when they sit, hunching their shoulders protecting their hearts from being vulnerable. Do they sit upright, exposing their chest to exude confidence with themselves? Does he take you in with eye contact? Are his hips aligned directly toward yours when speaking? Use your senses, guys! Be expressive toward women, who can be like telephones. Punch the wrong button, and you get disconnected… but dial the right connection, and you will open up a sexual volcano.

In the pursuit of a new relationship, people who have had a healthy relationship with their own sexual past are usually able to bring that into the bedroom for the future. But people who have feelings of shame around sex usually have issues around intimacy. People who don't need intimacy and have none (even if it has to be with oneself) usually end up becoming like the Unabomber, hiding out in the mountains somewhere. Men, in talking about their pasts, are generally comfortable with themselves. If they have been enriched by their experiences, all the better for you; but if they are secretive about other relationships, then there is something they don't want you to know. If you get naked and jump in the sack, you will find out soon enough.

One last thing… there is a natural order of things that are dealt with by everybody who is in the mood. Great sex is not a neat and tidy, sterile affair. It gets messy, and guess what, it should! If your date has a habit of sending back the silverware in a restaurant, worries about germs on the doorknobs, or screams every time they see a bug, you might have a problem and be disappointed. There is nothing less sexy than anxiety, which is definitely a turn-off. Everyone gets a little nervous at times, but if there is a degree that is borderline obsessive, how can you feel free and let your guard down? How can there be an emotional communication if someone has to jump up quickly to shower (unless it's together of course)? Getting down and dirty is part of great sex. There is a reason for a messy-hair look: it's sexy! So, leave your hair on the tousled side, wear your shirt untucked, and don't worry about spilling a little sauce now and then.

MIDNIGHT DISC JOCKEY

I had just gotten my divorce and was out celebrating at a *Jezebel Magazine* party. Bored to tears, gazing around I noticed this stud—he was 6'4" and a very attractive, and someone I had seen online. He was a disc jockey at one of the local radio stations. He noticed me as well and came over to engage in conversation. We connected, and he asked me out to dinner. *Sure, why not?* I thought. *A rock and roll DJ is probably a lot of fun.* He had very polite manners and called me the next day with our reservations for Friday at Agave in Midtown.

It was a lot of fun. The owners came out and were very attentive, bringing us special appetizers, loaded potent margaritas, and then tequila shooters. My Spanish was getting better, and we were having a great time. He asked if I wanted to go dancing, but I declined. It was late, so he took me home. When we arrived at my place, I asked him if he wanted to come in for a drink, but warned him that the only thing in the bar was scotch.

"Sure," he said. "Scotch is fine, but that's a pretty strong drink for a petite blonde," he joked.

I hope he's not thinking I'm trying to seduce him, I thought.

"Uh, just scotch on ice?" he asked.

"I'm out of soda, too. Would you like water with it?" I asked.

"No, no. That's great. Just bring it on," he said.

We drank and continued to talk. I was trying to find some great music for a DJ, so I flipped in the Rolling Stones.

"Do you smoke marijuana?" he asked.

Since my date from the night before had actually left some, I said, "Sure. I've actually got some in that little drawer in the coffee table." We lit up a joint to "If You Can't Get What You Want, Get What Ya Need" and puffed away. He started to make a move on me because I'm sure the weed made him horny (or maybe the scotch made him brave), but I just wasn't feeling the chemistry. While we were making out on the couch, my miniature Chihuahua Pluto jumped up and tried to bite his face off. Obviously, the dog could sense that I wasn't interested and felt intruded upon. My little four-pound guardian angel!

He suddenly then turns with a weird look and said, "If I were to feel strange, where is the nearest hospital?"

"What do you mean by strange?" I asked, assuming he was paranoid or something of the sort.

"Where would you take me?" he asked.

"What are you taking about? I mean, I guess North Side or Grady," I answered, all the while wondering what in the world was wrong with him.

"I'm not feeling well, like my heart or something. Can you take me to the nearest hospital?" he asked.

With glazed eyes, I answered, "Uh, okay. Why don't I just drive you home, and then I will take a taxi back to my place?"

"No I already feel motion sick. Call 9-1-1. I feel like I am going to have a heart attack," he said, his voice raising. I gave him a Coke and a wet towel and made the call.

The dispatcher asked for his name, so I gave his radio name. "No! That is not my real name!" he yelled, still paranoid.

"Well, I don't know who you are. What is your name?" I said in a panic. *God, I've got to get this drug paraphernalia out of here!* I ran over to the neighbor's yard and ditched it. Two Cobb County fire trucks came screeching down my street, waking the neighbors.

"Ma'am, what's the problem?" they asked as they hook up some kind of machine to his heart. "Sir, what have you been drinking? Have you been drinking any alcohol?" they asked.

"Uh, yeah. We had dinner and a lot of margaritas, some tequila shooters, and two scotch on the rocks," he said.

With raised eyebrow, the EMT asked, "Have you had anything else?"

"Well, yes. There was some marijuana my date gave to me," he said. I was ready to shoot him right then and there!

"When's the last time you smoked pot, sir?" asked the paramedic.

"About fifteen years ago," he blurted out.

"Your heart is fine, but I think you just need to stay here tonight," he said as they packed up to leave.

Oh my God, I thought. *I'm 5'4', 100 pounds soaking wet, and he is 6'4", twice my weight and is tripping out trying to be the big cool dude mixing too much alcohol and pot and can't handle it. I could go to jail over this!* He ran into the bathroom to puke.

"Hey, listen… you can sleep in my guest room. I will keep the door unlocked and the alarm off in case you are able to go home later," I said.

The next morning, I got up and he was gone. Thank God I didn't have to face him! I called down to the radio station to see if he was okay and got him on the phone.

"What did you give me last night, some kind of pot laced with another drug of some kind?" he asked. "I know sometimes you women will do something like that just to get

LAID." What nerve! I never listened to his radio show after that!

Mimi in Atlanta, Georgia

THE SEX KITTEN THAT SCREWED ME

I remember a girl who I met online. We corresponded with one another, and she finally wrote, "You look so crazy and so fun. If you look anything like your picture, I have to see you!" (I am not arrogant, by the way).

I decided to have her come to my house instead of meeting for a measly dinner. She strutted into my home wearing a low-cut top, provocatively displaying most of her beasts. She was undeniably attractive and beautiful in many different and essential ways. I dashed over fearlessly and give her an enormous bear hug! The next thing I knew, she was kissing me very passionately with her tongue gently at first and then roughly. I was really enjoying this and hoping there would be more! I thought, *Let's skip the getting to know each other and move on to the next best thing.*

The next thing I can recall is that we were in my kitchen having a martini. Within two minutes, her breasts were out in the open, and she was on my expensive countertop. She then stooped down on my Brazilian hardwood floor and told me to come closer to her, exclaiming "God, I love this! You are just... just amazing."

I said, "Baby, you don't have to do that."

"What do you mean? I do have to do it. I want to do it," she insisted.

The next thing I knew, we were laying on the hardwood floor. She screamed out, "I just met you! Oh my God, I feel like I know you. Love me, baby!"

I said, "Baby, I don't even do this myself."

She answered, "Well, do it now!" and we did. We spent three days together. We hardly left my bedroom, and it was just splendid. That was our first date, and it was so unbelievably worth it.

I actually did start to love the girl. We dated three vivacious months, and it didn't work out because she wasn't who I thought she was. Little did I know she was actually on the *Jerry Springer* show! She was unbelievable drama and would constantly cry during arbitrary moments about the most insignificant things. She cheated on me occasionally and lied consistently. She was quadruple dipping with me, half of a dip with her ex-boyfriend. She would see him once a month while seeing me all the time. I came to the conclusion that a lot of women are this way and think it's okay, but it's not—even if 75 to 80 percent of the American population could easily be on Jerry Springer's guest list.

John in Las Vegas, Nevada

> *John, unfortunately you were the victim of a Love Addict. These people feed off the drama and excitement that the beginnings of relationships provide. However, they are not able to maintain this level of stimulation for long and often will cause very dramatic scenes as to cause a riff. Most love addicts have a deep underlying fear of intimacy, and as such—when it comes close, they go running. Feel grateful and thank your lucky stars that this girl did you the favor of leaving before she became more toxic to your life. Remember for the future, what starts fast—usually ends fast.*

THE TALE OF THE HORNY TIGHTWAD

The tale I'm about to tell is a story that you just can't make up. This is a tale of greed, lust, and deception. Listen carefully, because these guys are out there, and not just in the confines of L.A.'s glitter-filled avenues. They might be in your own backyard. This particular dude was one of the most alarming presentations I have witnessed in my short, but substantive dating career in L.A. His Match.com profile should have been my tip-off. In it, he shares, "Sex is very important to me. I'm not saying it has to be the entire relationship, but I was just in a relationship for three years, and it was dead."

Okay, there was a red flag, but like all women set on finding Mr. Right and compromising their own gut feelings, I reasoned, "Okay. Maybe he is just a really good communicator, and what psychologist doesn't want that?" I responded to the ad, and he asked for my number within the next email. I gave it to him, and we spoke for a few moments (never reveal too much on the phone or you'll have nothing to talk about on the date) and agreed to meet the following week when I got back into L.A.

The week I returned, I received a call from him around ten thirty p.m. Now, after reading The Rules, I know to never even pick up the phone when a guy calls this late, but this was months ago. I picked up, and after chatting briefly, he asked if I would like to "Come over [his] way." Ladies, this should have been red flag number two! Any guy worth his salt is not going to call at ten thirty at night and expect you to drop everything and come to HIM! Even pre-rules, I declined and told him that I would prefer to meet him at a public place, close to my apartment. I suggested a casual bar that was down the road, and he huffed, "I don't drink alcohol, and bars are for alcoholics."

At this point, it should have been "STRIKE THREE. YOU'RE OUT, BUDDY!" and I should have ended the call right there. However, not missing a beat in my little sugar-coated mind, I reasoned *Hmm... a guy that doesn't drink... now that's kind of refreshing.* We met at Coffee Shop 101 out on the street, and he stopped mid-walk and exclaimed, "You are absolutely beautiful." He said it with such genuine honesty, such disbelief, as though he had not seen forty-three other blue-eyed blondes in L.A. that previous day.

When we got the check, he looked at it and then at me as if I was supposed to partake in some new-age going-Dutch approach. Bear in mind that total amounted to a big bad $7.53, as we only split dessert. I stared blankly back at him until he realized this was not going to happen. He paid, and I thanked him. Exasperated, he responded, "Thank you for saying that. You have no idea how many girls don't even say thanks."

As the night came to an end, he suggested we go back to my place so he could "check out [my] website," but I am no dummy. I remembered all too well that this one had said, "Sex is very important to me" in his Match.com profile. However, being the nice girl that I am, I obliged, knowing (a) that I had two somewhat large male roommates if he turned out to be a psycho killer, and (b) this would help me know really quickly whether or not to see him again if he came on too strong.

When we get there, he had his man-bag handy. He made a beeline for my bathroom and took out his contacts and puts on his glasses. I began to wonder if he was going to start doing the crossword in the *New York Times* and make himself more at home—in MY home. I thought, *this is a little strange, but whatever. This guy has not had the luxury of having alcohol smoothly guide his impulses, and so he is just a bit quirky.*

Quirky indeed! There was a bit of chitchat and then BANG, he planted one right on the kisser! As any hot-blooded female, at a sub-conscious level, I enjoyed this very aggressive male approach. However, my warning system had been activated and I noted that he only brought the man-bag because he was planning on staying the night. I stopped him right before he struck out again on the wrong base. I ever so graciously thanked him and hinted that I was tired and had a big day and so on and so forth.

He called the next day to say he had "a great time" and would like to see me again. This time, he suggested that I bring my swimsuit, because he had a pool at his place—I wanted to remind him that in L.A., everyone has a pool, but I didn't. He used a text message to ask me out this time, a cowardly way for men to suggest things they will probably be rebuffed for, and I did not respond. An hour later, he texted "You might as well bring your PJs over as well." I promptly responded that I did not have a good feeling and wanted to cancel. He immediately called and apologized, saying, "Texts never relate joking humor." I basically was over him by this point, even if he didn't realize it.

Fast forward three weeks, and he called and asked to go out again. I asked where, and he said, "I don't know. Just out someplace" I thought, *Okay, maybe he is coming around.* If you are wondering by now why on earth I would give him a third chance, it is because I am a hopeless romantic and always root for the underdog. What if this guy made a complete turnaround? Not to mention he was 6'5" and looked like a cocktail of David Duchovny and Zach Braff.

So, we agreed upon a night to meet. Having not heard anything from him by six thirty, I texted, "Uh… are we still going out?" I got no response for a long time, and when he did finally answer, all it said was that he was napping and hadn't made plans as of yet.

I texted back, "I'm really confused. You asked me out for Tuesday last week."

He responded, "Yeah, sorry. I was in a daze. Literally just woke up when you texted. You wanna come this way? Got anything you want to do?" When I told him that I could come that way, and he needed to just name the place, he answered,

"Hmm... my place? I don't know what to do plan-wise. Watching my money. Got any ideas?"

I didn't give up on him just yet. I said, "Well, I'm not really sure what there is around your area. Let me look and see if there is a restaurant close by that looks cool."

"Sorry if I wasn't clear. I'll join you at a restaurant, but I don't have the extra money to pay for anything right now."

My last response was, "I appreciate the honest communication, so let me reciprocate... I don't' think you can afford me. Best of luck to you."

Colleen in Los Angeles, California

It sounds so cliché, but the truth is women want a relationship and sometimes men are mostly interested in getting their physical needs met (not necessarily a relationship). I have heard many men say they have a lot of patience and tolerance when the sex is "out if this world." Steve Harvey is right when he expounds on how men assess what is required to attain a particular woman, and how to keep her. Women should have standards and expect a man to make effort for them. If they are not up for the challenge, send them off to pluck the lower hanging fruit.

THE LIBRARIAN

I met this lady online whom I had an obtuse attraction for. She was 5'9", voluptuous, and discreetly beautiful behind the glasses and swept-up hair. We emailed back and forth, spoke on the phone, and decided to meet. However, being the adventurous, radical, yet sophisticated European, I decide to create a very nice picnic lunch at a charming park halfway between us. Thus, at noon on a gorgeous sunny day in early October, we had our first date.

I prepared a medley of Mediterranean baked appetizers, expansive Sausalito salad, and strawberries and cream, washed down with a mix of green tea and ginger ale. Upon meeting her, I realized that she looked just like her profile picture, which was a plus—very much like Sarah Palin. While she was walking toward me, I noticed that her grace and poise matched her librarian look exquisitely, like something out of a graceful silent movie. I couldn't help but fantasize, but I had to drop this distraction before I dropped our lunch! She walked up carrying a book in her hand. I greeted her and said, "Lovely day! I booked it in advance at great expense!"

She said, "Since you are a musician, I thought that you would enjoy this great book on Woodstock. We can flip through it while we have lunch." We walked with our picnic lunch, and she selected a surprisingly private spot where we could talk further, enjoy the scenery, and eat. While discussing Woodstock with her, I noticed that she seemed very shy and introverted but very open about her life in a very soft-spoken, calm, and collected way. We flipped through the pages of the book in the midst of a beautiful day when an alternating experience occurred. She took off her glasses and gave me a seductive, buoyant look. Her disposition changed tremendously. Her personality switched from introverted and austere to flirtatious, carefree, and aggressive. She immediately stood up exclaiming, "Oh, dear! My jeans are somehow wet from the damp grass!" She then removed them casually, laying them on a nearby rock in the sun.

Consequently, she stood there in only a top and panties, which seemed a bit strange and awkward due to the circumstances. I thought it was best to diffuse the situation by pretending to check my own and found I had the same wet issue and dropped my pants as well. I honestly thought this equality would make her feel more comfortable. I thought, *Okay, here we both our in our underwear in a public park in the middle of the day. How much weirder could this situation get?* Just when I thought the situation couldn't get any more awkward, she began to unbutton her top, exposing her bra and breasts. I couldn't resist kissing her; I am male, after all. Immediately, she pounced on me like a lioness in heat! It wasn't a mild sexual overture—but a lioness going for the kill. We immediately start having mad sex on a blanket in the middle of the day at this public park. We had uncontrollable sex for two hours in a private undiscovered little cove. After this encounter, she instantly threw her glasses back on her face. She gave me a timid and embarrassed look for losing her composure. She said, "I'm so sorry. I don't know what has come over me. This has all been too surreal and blurry. I uh… I think the pages of the book that I was flipping through must have been laced with LSD or something. I have no other explanation. I just don't know what… I uh… have done!"

Of course, being the gentleman that I am, I assured her that everything that happened was fine. I said, "We have enjoyed a beautiful afternoon in the park, that's all." We both awkwardly zipped up our pants. I then walked her back to her car, and she seemed to have a completely changed demeanor. Nothing was said, and she drove away. I never saw her or heard from her again. I concluded that she must have some sort of Clark Kent syndrome. Behind the glasses was an alter ego, which explained her strange but highly enjoyable behavior on a gorgeous day at the public park.

<u>Bob in London, United Kingdom</u>

DR. BOOTY CALL

I met "Sam" through Match.com. His profile said he was looking for a level-headed and independent woman, and that he had a Ph.D. To top all of this off, he was also from the Midwest and was absolutely gorgeous—curly brown hair, light green eyes, triathlon physical condition, and a killer smile to match. I was already calling the chapel. I decided to give him my cell number, and we continued to banter on for about thirty minutes between texts, most of it a mixture of Will Ferrell lines (which he scored major Brownie points for) and telling me "Your eyes are gorgeous, by the way." Enough said.

The next day, he texted and asked if I wanted to meet for a drink. Female translation: *This guy is not completely sure about you. Otherwise, he would invest the time and money for a dinner.* However, later he suggested dinner and said he would call. Although he called on the same day for a dinner date, I couldn't resist. What if this guy was just as stoked about me as I was of him and also couldn't wait to meet? We set up dinner for the following evening.

Seven thirty arrived and so did I to his apartment (again, another rules no-no of driving to the guy for the first couple dates, but I honestly never have an excuse to get out by the beach). He said "I think I see you, if you're that gorgeous lady walking through the parking lot in a red dress." We greeted with a peck and hug (usual Cali formalities) and began walking. I was immediately smitten. He was gorgeous! His eyes were light green and quite pretty for a guy. His teeth were perfect, with the slightest little gap in the middle. We ended up sitting on the porch having some very deep conversations about family and politics. He had a great job—and did I mention that he was gorgeous? I definitely had butterflies!

He showed me pictures of his nieces and nephews, which were placed around his house. This was a sign to me that he valued family. He told me that he moved to Santa Monica because there was not a very good dating scene where he used to live. This told me he valued relationships. He talked of his job and told me that he wanted to be "a good dad and be at all of [his] kids' soccer games." This won me over. This guy couldn't have been more of a package if he was wrapped in a shiny box and matching bow. We walked to dinner and ate at some overpriced Mexican joint, though I could have sat with this guy at McDonald's for all I cared. It was truly one of those dates where the world around you seems to dissolve, and I hoped the night would never end.

We went back to his place and had another beer. I used the bathroom and found him just standing in his living room. I walked up to him, and we kissed. There was no build-up, no anticipation, and no hesitation—it just happened like it was supposed to happen. He jokingly told me that he wanted to do that the minute we met but was afraid it might be too soon. I'm pretty sure any moment of the night would have been fine with me. It was a good few hours of making out and doing things that one should not do on a first date. By the next morning, the rulebook was completely thrown out the window. I thought, *this guy has a Ph.D., Colleen. He is completely into you and is a bit more evolved than the ole rules gals would have you believe. Besides, do you want a guy that likes you for you, spontaneous and free, or a guy that likes you for who he idealizes you to be, masked by the archaic behaviors that The Rules prescribes?*

He texted me the next day. The message said, "I just wanted to tell you I had a great time with you last night." *Yes, Sam, I bet you did.* However, I knew this was guy code, for "I'm into you…

otherwise, I wouldn't have bothered." He left for a trip to Vegas with his buddies, and texted me later that night with a simple "I'm a fan of you." I was not a fan of this behavior.

There was no call all day, and a text past ten thirty that simply stated he was a "fan"? A fan of what, sleeping with me? By now, you have probably guessed that our friend Sam was not a phone person. He suffered from "phonophobia," an epidemic-affecting males between fourteen and thirty-nine. The next time he attempted to ask me out was via text, upon which he was promptly rebuffed. I told him that I would prefer to be asked out the old-fashioned way and that he needed to call. He called, and we made plans for Saturday night. That wasn't that bad at all. He called on Wednesday for a Saturday night date! In the meantime, we texted back and forth. I was getting the closest thing to a relationship this guy knew how to offer. Albeit digital, my little heart always skipped a beat when I heard the magical chime of my iPhone and knew it was him.

After a couple of days, I received no text messages or calls. I got no response. Nothing. Nada. For twelve painful hours. His response the next day was "Holla... you too... give you a call later tonight." It was painful to say the least. To my surprise, he did actually call and leave a message: "Hey, Colleen, its Dr. Van Kamp (he said this jokingly of course, as he wasn't that narcissistic). Just wanted to see if we might be able to reschedule for Saturday. A good friend of mine is coming in Saturday, and I'm wondering if we could reschedule for during the day." It was official. I showed my hand a bit too early, and I had been downgraded to a day date. I agreed to the friggin day date, and of course, got a booty call the night before (that I did not answer). I was now one of *those* girls.

We met and walked around Santa Monica. I noticed his body language was different. He was no longer leaning toward me. When he talked, he looked around me and over my shoulder. He was no longer fixing his gaze on me as he did the first date. He would pat my back like we were good buddies vs. on a date. When I explained to him that I interpreted his rescheduling our date as a sign that he was not that interested, he just remained silent vs. trying to counter my argument.

Another week went by and I had not heard a word—not even a text—from good ole Dr. Sam. Greg Behrendt. This definitely says "He's just not that into you, Colleen," and I am aware of this. As the days go by, the sting of rejection dissipates. Although my ego is a bit bruised, I still have not lost faith that somewhere in our world of six billion people, there is one out there just as great as Sam who will think the same thing about me.

Colleen in Los Angeles, California

Imagine our grandmothers getting a booty call! Thank god we've come a long way from barefoot, pregnant, to birth control, fulfilling careers, and economic independence. Regardless of our empowerment, the innate primal trait of maleness seems to escape evolution know matter what era you put him in. Perhaps electrical shocks when such attempts are made would curb the "booty call" impulse. The Queen of Soul, Aretha Franklin, sums it up best, R-E-S-P-E-C-T and for women the burden is often on us to demand it.

CHAPTER 3

OH, MY DATE LIED.
WHAT A SURPRISE!

Have you ever been disappointed to see a car lift by three feet when your date steps out of the car? The big, big hunk of burning love just does not resemble the photo or the "fit and trim" selection on their profile. What about finally meeting the handsome fantasy salt-and-pepper haired gentleman only to find out that there is no pepper—just salt and dentures and a cane that never appeared on the pictures they posted, most of which were taken at least a decade ago. What about the date who says, "No, really, I AM divorced" and leads you on, forgetting to mention that while they have been divorced, they are NOW married to someone else. The cyber world of anonymity holds not only "little white lies," but also some really big lies that can be highly disappointing. The biggest complaint with online dating is deception. You can't pull the wool over someone's eyes for very long before your discovered, especially if you meet someone you really like. Honesty is the best policy!

Post a current photo.

Don't post a picture of your dog, cat, or bird. No one wants to date your pet! Live in the present with a good quality picture of yourself dressed nicely, guys—not one taken with your cell phone on the bathroom mirror reflecting your shirtless torso. Yes, women want to see your muscles, but in due time. Whether you are bald, overweight, or underweight, it's who you are, and there is someone out there that is interested in you!

Write an interesting profile.

Tell a story of who you are, not of who you would like to be. People are reading profiles to get a sense of personality and of the entire package of the person (not just the physical features). Expound on your experiences or what makes you unique from others. Less is better than a dissertation. Remember, there are other profiles of interest online. You have a paragraph or two to catch their attention.

List your real age.

The most common lie online is about age. A majority of people put down the age their friends tell them they look like. Yes, we all want to be sure we make it past the cut off for age criteria, but you run the risk of mistrust if you meet someone you want to pursue. We have heard stories where both men and women are lying by ten years or more! Even facelifts will not hide the truth!

Be truthful about your body type and height.

The first red flag is only one photo from the neck up and not a full body picture. Helloooo! Men complain the most about women not revealing their true size. Let it all hang out! If someone is not interested, there are plenty of fish in the sea. Women complain about men lying about their height. If you are 5'9" and say you are 6'0", they will find out the truth when you meet—and you don't want to have to wear platform shoes on your first date, guys!

Everyone has plenty of people who are attracted to the person you are. You don't have to be a certain type! **PLEASE JUST BE HONEST. IT WILL SAVE YOU MONEY, TIME, AND EMBARRASSMENT!**

MEN ARE FROM STUPID, WOMEN ARE FROM SNEAKY

I met my second wife on Yahoo personals. I wasn't ready. I hadn't been divorced long enough. I trapped myself pretty good because our engagement was really public. She was not the first person that I dated, but it was the first serious relationship. We met online and dated about nine months before we got married. We got engaged pretty quickly, and then I felt kind of stuck. We were married for thirteen months. It took a few years to divorce her. We got engaged at the Governor's mansion, at his Christmas party. The next morning, someone called in at Q100 radio and told the story of our engagement. So everyone I knew also knew about it. I kept trying to excuse her issues and problems, but a few months after we got engaged. She was having problems with her ex and son. Her lawyer wasn't doing a very good job, so my father found another lawyer. He went and got her file and said, "I think I can wrap this thing up in two weeks." That was the good news. The bad news is that I had gotten engaged at the Governor's mansion and married a MARRIED woman—in front of everybody.

She claimed that she had a misunderstanding with her spouse in Kentucky and had not resolved child custody or marital assets. She also claimed that she had a misunderstanding with her attorney. But after all I went through with her; I can almost assume that all of these were lies. I believe she knew she was still technically married and kept it a secret. I don't think she expected me to propose when I did. She was on the spot and accepted, knowing full well that she shouldn't.

The attorney wrapped up the divorce, and I ended up getting a lot of warning signs. When she didn't get her way, she lost her temper. She always tried to force her way, and she would not give up until she had it. It was a nightmare from the beginning, but it only got worse when she lost her job right after we got married. Things got really bad then. I couldn't get her to get another job. She was suing her employer for wrongful termination. She actually had a case because they fired her for refusing to violate affirmative action laws and do illegal background checks. She would not look for anything else and was draining me financially. She wasn't afraid to tell me, "Look… you need to get it through your head. You're gonna pay my bills. I am NEVER gonna work again. You're gonna pay my bills, and that's just the way it is. That's your lot in life. The sooner you accept it, the happier we'll both be."

When I met her, she was an executive of a Fortune 500 company. I thought we were extremely well matched, but she had an agenda. She took over our finances. I let her because she was at home and had time to mess with it. When we split up and I took my checkbook back and started going through there, it showed that she made six payments a month on her bills and one on mine. It was a nightmare. I was her fourth husband. She told me that all of the men in her life had always been mean and abusive—that they were drunks and the like. I said to her, "Well, we're going to be getting along great, because I am a nice guy. I honestly believe that." I am here to tell you that if that woman married Gandhi, it wouldn't have been long before Gandhi went to jail for domestic violence.

We broke up, and I got the ring back. A week or two later, she called crying and begging me to understand and promised she would never bribe me; it just looked that way. She said she just couldn't stand losing me, and I ended up taking her back. I loved her, but I didn't realize at the time that she was not "the one." I didn't realize that she had all these issues, especially with the men in her life. The lowest common denominator was her. She was a pro at getting divorced. I noticed this toward the end of the marriage, when I started talking seriously about divorcing her. She started planning her strategies for it. Finally, one day I told her, "I want you to pack your stuff and get out of my house."

She responded, "Oh, I won't be going anywhere. YOU will!"

"What are you talking about?" I asked. "This is my house. This is premarital property, and you are not on the deed."

"Well, it doesn't matter. You're gonna be leaving for domestic violence," she replied.

"What? I have never laid a hand on you!" I responded.

"I know, but try to convince the judge of that when he sees my videotape," she threatened.

"What videotape?"

"Wouldn't you like to know?" she said.

Finally, I managed to find one of the videotapes, and I realized she had recorded many of the arguments and fights between us. When I realized how bad things were getting, I tried to rectify the situation. "Let's just go to the mountains. Let's just chill and have a good time. Let's stop all this," I suggested.

We went to the mountains, but things didn't change. We argued all the way there and back. So when I got home, I said, "You know what? I am going to the video store to rent *Fantastic Four*. I've been waiting to see it, and I'm going to get a bottle of wine. I am gonna come back and sit down in my favorite chair, and I am gonna watch my movie and drink my wine, and I don't want anyone bothering me for two hours." About halfway through my movie, unbeknownst to me at the time, she set up her Sony digital video camera to record. She then came downstairs, walked over to the DVD player, ejected the DVD I was watching, and hurled it as far out into the woods as she could like a Frisbee. I just watched her with my jaw hanging down in sheer disbelief. She then went upstairs, laid down on the bed and waited. Meanwhile I was outside in twenty-degree weather, in the pitch black, barefoot, searching feverishly for the rented DVD—and getting madder and madder every second. I dug through wet bushes and prickly briers and still never found that DVD. When I came back into the house, I was livid, and understandably so. I rushed upstairs and verbally let her have it. I was furious! But instead of fighting back or arguing, she just lay there quietly, looking up at the camera every now and then as if she was about to cry.

She had made half a dozen videos like that. Toward the end of the marriage, she actually went to my employees and my assistant, Abby, whom I've been working with for ten years. She tried to convince Abby that my family and my neighbors, and my church, and my friends, and her were all going to get together and have an intervention and have me committed somewhere for anger management. She told Abby she was going to be taking over and offered Abby a 30 percent cut if she would help her out. One day as I was leaving work, Abby asked to meet with me. "Mark," she said, "can I talk to you for a minute?" Abby's mother worked for me part-time, and she was there as well. They came in my office and Abby held up a tape recorder.

"What's that for?"

"Well, I have something I need to talk to you about, and I just think we should have a tape recorder here for this conversation."

I responded accordingly, "Okay, go ahead."

She told me what my wife had said to her, and I explained, "Abby, I need you to understand. This second marriage of mine is a DISASTER. It's not going to work. We're gonna be splitting up. What she is doing here is basically trying to lay out the framework for a divorce fight."

Abby replied, "Oh, thank God!" Then she started telling me the rest of the details. My wife wanted to have me put away while she controlled my company. Basically, she was trying to convince my employees to turn on me so she could go to a judge and say, "His employees have even turned on him."

When I told her I was going to get a divorce, she beat me to it. She found the meanest female lawyer divorce attorney in Gwinnett County. She ran up my credit card with this woman and kept her until she realized she didn't have any money to pay her with, and then she dumped her. For whatever reason, she finally gave up. It was a nightmare, but I finally settled with her. The thing is, when we got married, she had a lot of debt that I rolled over to lower the interest rates. I didn't realize it, but from a legal perspective, I assumed her debt. Even after thirteen months, I was stuck with her debt afterwards. When we split up, I said, "Look, we've only been married thirteen months. I pay my debt and you pay your debt," but she wouldn't hear of it.

She said, "No, I am not paying my debt. You're stuck with it."

The marriage cost me $160,000, but I guess you live and learn. I can always make more money, but my main concern is falling for the wrong wife. I don't believe in bitterness, because if you let that grow then it will invade every aspect of your life. There ARE people with principles and morals and ethics out there. But it's like stepping off the Grand Canyon… you just might fall, and that's exactly what happened to me! You just gotta laugh, move on, and get past it!

Mark in Atlanta, Georgia

This story is a true testimony to the idea that love knows no limits, especially when it comes to stupidity. To not check on your finances for years, while your wife only made one payment toward your debt while making six payments a month towards her own is just pure ineptitude. Just because, you merge as a couple, does not mean you lose your independence, yourself, or your mind, as in Mark's case. If you find yourself in these types of horrible scenarios with predator companions over and over again— it may be a fair question to ask yourself—"who is the common denominator?" Love can be a very powerful and wonderful emotion, just make sure it is a two-way street before making the leap. A little accountability builds trust and can set the path towards a great relationship. At the very least, it will help you see the train wreck coming.

THE HUSTLER WITH THE SILVER TOUNGUE

I started online dating, going on dates with men in the depths of New York City. I grew up in Manhattan and am pretty savvy about most people. I am in business and have been in sales, so I am very quite intuitive. However, I don't think any of it helped me regarding the online dating routine of men. A while ago, I was in the process of divorcing and therefore was not looking online for someone to marry. I do believe, still, as a single woman that I am attractive for my age.

I was contacted by a man online who was a little bit younger than me. He had an MBA and another master's in a very technical area that had to do with financial marketing at one of the top universities in New York. During the first date, I noticed that he was so aristocratic and good-looking. He kind of resembled Harry Connik, Jr. He was the kind of guy that always had a suit and tie on. He had a look that wasn't a conventional pretty boy look, but a very engaging, attractive look with extreme sophistication. I felt a very strong, intense physical connection with the man. It was very unusual, as I do not have such a vital sense of chemistry with many people. He wasn't tremendously handsome but was quite charismatic. What made him so attractive was his power of being so persuasive and eloquent. He definitely had the gift of the silver tongue.

On the second date, he seemed so intuitive and poignant. It seemed like he knew exactly what kind of a man a woman wants and what women typically think about. It was almost like a scene from *What Women Want* with Mel Gibson, except this was real not a movie.

On the third date, he asked me to meet him at an amusing restaurant but not exactly impressive in a woman's eyes. Although the restaurant was very well known, it is one of those places men usually go after work to hang out, sit at the bar, and watch the games. Since I don't even work in mid-town, the location was not completely in my direction, but I had a feeling that he wanted to show me off to his guy buddies. I believed that the restaurant was certainly not a place where he would have taken me to dinner. He implied it, but I just knew that he wouldn't. I went over there, and sure enough there were a bunch of guys ready to ogle me. I was there briefly and we left together and arrived at a very delightful gourmet restaurant. The restaurant wasn't as crowded, which seemed so much more enjoyable because we had a chance to converse a little more.

Then he said to me out of nowhere, "You know, I have a friend who is in the Mafia."

I said to myself, "Well, that's encouraging. GREAT!"

And then he said, "I really think that he would like you." His statement sent a shock up my spine. What was this man talking about?

I replied, "Why are you telling me this?"

"Well, he just broke up with his girlfriend of many years, and he is very, very wealthy, and I know you're having financial trouble."

I said, "I am going through a divorce."

"Well," he said, "I just, thought... he tends to really like women who are very bright, beautiful, and articulate. I think that he would really like you."

I said, "I don't understand, but why are you telling me this? We are on a date. We are on a third date. Why would you bring this up?"

He went on to say, "Well, you know, it would be a win-win situation because you need some help financially and, uh... it turns out that this guy left his ex girlfriend a beautiful condo and stash in the bank. He really likes to take care of his girlfriends. He stays in committed relationships for years. He really treats his girlfriend right. There is one peculiar thing though... he likes watching his girlfriend having sex with other men that he really knows and likes, which is where I come in."

I thought to myself, *that's a win-win situation?* I was so shocked, in spite of being a New Yorker. But nothing like this had ever, ever happened to me! This was so out of the blue... I was really not only shocked, but also disappointed. After three dates, I had begun to think there was something good going on, and then he revealed this! A friend in the Mafia? Voyeurism and wild sex? All I could say to him when he told me about it was, "Sounds interesting." After such a shocking conversation, the dinner seemed a bit awkward and tense, and I was glad it was coming to an end. I was sure he noticed that I had become a bit withdrawn during dinner because he never called me back for a fourth date.

Later on, I realized the whole thing was rather bizarre, considering I have never been the kind of person who works for benefits in relationships. I have always taken care of myself, always made my own way. I even put my ex-husband through school! I am not one of the New Yorkers that thinks about dating only the big time moneymakers, and I am not materialistic. If he had listened to me at all in our many conversations, he would have known this. I began to wonder how many others he would have to ask before he found a taker. Was he just a con man whose job it was to find adequate girlfriends and wives for mafia men? It was a disappointing, shocking experience, but I'll know a con man the next time I see one.

Katherine in Manhattan, New York

Unfortunately, the Internet is a mysterious medium popular with predators looking for opportunity. Even a mafia gofer will eventually find a willing participant. I once had a lady admit she made a vast majority of her sales by networking online dates. If you run into a con, report an abuse or block them from contact.

THE FAT CAT

I had been online a couple of years and enjoyed the company of many gentlemen and also endured the company of many sleaze balls. However, I started chatting with one particular online man who had two head and shoulders pictures with a grin on his face. He had no other dazzling pictures to keep me interested, but his profile pointed out that he was slim, tall, and had a high income and a great career. In one picture, he had a baseball cap on his head. The other picture he had on his profile was another shoulder picture, but with the top of his head cut off! I thought to myself, *He must have a receding hairline, or maybe he's just plain bald!* He did look a bit attractive in the face, so I started talking to him on the phone for weeks and what seemed like hours at a time. I finally decided to meet him for afternoon lunch. *What's the harm in that?* I reasoned.

The day we decide to meet, I was sitting at the restaurant waiting for him, and he was late. The clock was ticking away, and I was getting impatient. *Maybe this just wasn't a good idea,* I thought as I sat beside the window so I could see him pull up and get a glimpse of who I was actually meeting. He finally pulled up and got out of his car, and I was completely and utterly SHOCKED! The car literally lifted up! He must have been a quarter-ton—at least 500 pounds. He was definitely not slim like it said on his profile, and he was completely bald. He came into the restaurant and opened his mouth to speak, only to reveal a mouthful of horrendous teeth that were so unkempt and rotted that they were about to fall out! I felt so sorry for the man because there was no chance of physical attraction whatsoever. When I finally met him, I felt like I had wasted hours getting to know him. I stayed for the lunch, but unlike his dishonesty, I decided to bite the bullet, be honest, and explain that I wasn't interested in dating him. He seemed extremely bitter and angry about it. It was a very uncomfortable situation. I ended up paying the tab for my half of brunch and saying goodbye to Mr. Fat Cat!

Christie in Atlanta, Georgia

I must say, unfortunately, this type of date happens more often than not. The man lies about his financial status, the woman lies about her age. I never quite understood why people do this. Is the assumption that, although you've gained the weight of a small child, you are simply going to gloss over that with your sparkling personality? This kind of behavior is a red flag. If

someone is willing to start off a relationship with a lie—
it probably won't be the last!

CYBER RAGE AND DEUCE GIGALO

There I was, sifting through men on the man menu, and I couldn't even find a decent appetizer. I got one email from a guy with a ponytail, shirtless photos, and a tattoo, to which I promptly clicked No Thanks and pressed send. Again the next week, he has the audacity to send me the same cut and paste message that he sent the week before. I wrote, "Dude, you're in Hawaii, and maybe your brain is fried from too much pot and sun exposure. You are way to tan for your age" I promptly clicked on Not Interested.

He wrote back, " Why don't you just block me? You're not getting any younger."

I couldn't resist responding. "Excuse me, but have you looked in the mirror lately? You're short and bald except for a strand in a ponytail. You are ten years older than me. I am HOT, so F—* off!"

Fortunately, the next email I got was from an amazing guy—a total package. We emailed back and forth and seemed to have a lot in common. When my girlfriend came over for a cocktail and I started chatting about this great guy and how he sends me poetry, what he does for a living, and so forth, she seemed startled. "Laura," she said, "the same man is sending me the same poetry and emails that he has sent to you!"

"WHAT?"

"Yes, but from a different site and user name."

"God, men are so stupid. Whatever. Let's invite him to my friend's party in Malibu, and we can both show up pretending neither of us knows he's been chatting us both up."

"Fabulous idea!"

The guy was completely lame. I invited him, and he met us at the party. We casually sandwiched him in between us and started a conversation. He obviously was too stupid to put two and two together. He turned to my friend and asked, "Uh, where do you live?"

"Why? Do you think I look familiar?" my friend asked.

"I don't know. Are you an actress?" he replied. In Hollywood, I guess that would be his first stupid guess.

She said, "Aren't you Bada Bing Bada Bing? Wait a minute. You are that guy who was chatting me up who couldn't wait to go out," my friend said.

Right away, it clicked. "Oh my God! That is my SugarDaddy. com name."

"Oh, and you sent me the same poetry you sent my friend under fun4u at Match.com."

The renegade pimp a—* was caught red handed and the jig was up! He proceeded to get really drunk while we continued mingling with others. He didn't even attempt to apologize, so we just left him there drunk, embarrassed, exposed, and pathetic. Plus, we told all our other girlfriends that were on the same site all about him. Moral of the story: "You play, you pay!"

Laura in Malibu, California

RELIGION AND DECEPTION

I met a guy online and loved his profile, although I am not really religious and he was Jewish. We chatted consistently, spoke on the phone, and decided to briefly meet. He seemed like a really great guy, but I noticed that he did not have any kids and didn't seem to have much of a dating past. I found that a bit strange but continued to date him. I asked him about his business, and he told me that it was an Internet business selling Jewish memorabilia. He sold products such as menorahs and marriage certificates. He explained to me that he had another business but was never too specific.

We continued to date. He later showed me his gym and told me he worked out three to four times a week and would like me to work out with him more. I exclaimed, "I have a really hectic life with my kids, my career, and couldn't care less, to be honest! Trying to change people is a recipe for disaster." After that date, I had a gut feeling that there was something very strange about this guy, so I decide to Google him on the internet, and I find something totally shocking! The guy was a rabbi and owned his own synagogue! I wondered why he didn't mention this before.

The rabbi emailed me and said, "We haven't spoken in a week. Do you think we might be getting together?"

I tried to respond honestly about what was bothering me. "You never did mention that you are a rabbi. Is there a reason that you didn't tell me?"

He said, "It was the fact that you aren't Jewish or religious, and I don't agree with the things that you do with your life."

I retorted, "Well, I don't think lying is part of the religious equation, and I just don't think I am interested in people who are untrustworthy!"

I never saw the rabbi again!

Heidi in Manhattan, New York

THE BIG SURPRISE

About nine or ten years ago, I was a habitual online dater and had gone out with many women through gay.co.uk out of London. During a difficult period in my life, I turned to a chat room for support and wound up really falling for someone who was so nurturing that we hit it off. I was actually falling in love in a chat room. It is easy to do because chat rooms are very alluring and all consuming. Unlike real life, you get quick, instant messages without having to set up a date.

Anyway, I met this woman I'll call "Alex," who lived 2,000 miles away. After months of incessant emails and phone calls, we decided to have a rendezvous at a hotel midway between our respective locations. I booked my non-refundable plane ticket and made the hotel reservations. Then, a few weeks before our scheduled tryst, Alex sent me an email confessing a deep, dark secret. She was a transsexual! *What? She tells me now?* What was I supposed to do in that situation? I was beside myself. I was instantly turned off and obviously upset that she didn't alert me to this little piece of trivia before I made travel arrangements. Part of me really loved her for helping me through a difficult period in my life, even though we had chatted only through the phone and computer. I kept telling myself not to be so narrow-minded. I kept saying to myself, "You can do this. She is a woman now. What does the past matter? She's pretty in the pictures she sent."

Ultimately, I didn't want to be an a—hole, and the tickets were non-refundable, so I went. I was nervous as hell. I wish I could tell you we lived happily ever after, but this didn't turn out to be some progressive, gender bending romantic comedy. Male to female transsexuals are not all leggy cabaret stars. I just simply wasn't attracted to her, as open-minded as I was. She just looked manly—like a guy with long hair. Every attempt she made to appear feminine was undermined with terrible posture and general sloppiness. She just could not master the "girl thing." She wasn't even coming off as a butch lesbian. She was just a guy! I remember vividly when she was laying on top of me, looking down affectionately at me, and my mind kept saying *Man, woman, man, woman... man?* It was like a hologram. She had a post-operation, but it wasn't like the real thing. There was nothing she could do about those big hands, gangly feet, or her Adam's apple. She almost seemed suicidal, and I wished her luck, but honestly told her we were not the right fit.

Erica in London, United Kingdom

GORGEOUS CATCH A PENNY

Keep in mind that no matter how cute and sexy a guy is, there is always at least one woman somewhere who is sick of him. I thought, *why not push the recycle button and do what any other fifty-year-old woman with a vibrator and a toddler to care for would do... GET ONLINE!* While doing a search, I came across a man much too handsome to be interested in a fifty-year-old granny, so I continued searching. Being an amateur at most things Internet, I did not realize that others could see who had viewed their profiles. How scary is that? Mr. Gorgeous emailed me a few days later, and we started a dialogue. Eventually we were talking daily, and I was intrigued with the attention.

He said his birthday was the following week, so I offered to buy him dinner to celebrate. I had good vibes, so that weekend, I excitedly drove to his house. He wasn't home, so I waited.

This must not be the right neighborhood, I thought. I saw a car drive in. I was convinced that could not be his car, especially after reading about his high-profile career. The man walked over, and I pushed the lock down on my door. I turned, and his face was against my window.

"Put your window down," he said.

"Hell no! I don't know you," I said.

"Judy, it's me!" he screamed, verifying his screen name. In hindsight, I should have just floored the gas peddle.

We exchanged niceties and decided on a restaurant down the street. "I can't get over how beautiful you look. You look better than your pictures,'" he said.

"I can't get over how different you look than your pictures. How long ago were they taken?" I asked. (Eventually, I found out they were fifteen years old!) He then asked if he could drive my car to dinner because he was thinking of buying one himself. Not a bad idea, considering he was driving a 1978 Pontiac Fiero. I don't think he had ever seen a navigation system before. The drive was endless.

We pull up to the valet, and he said, "Hey, man, my car has a pushbutton starter. Can you operate that?" Horrified,

I walked into the Chinese restaurant thinking, *this should be quick, painless and cheap.*

"Would you like a drink?" he asked.

"I will have a glass of wine," I said.

He, of course, ordered a bottle of champagne. Immediately, my eyes start scanning for a back door to escape, but then again, the valet had my keys thinking it was his car. I was relatively trapped.

I run to the bathroom, and when I returned, I saw my date had already ordered. He said to me, "Baby, what would you like to order?"

Baby? Since when did we take the quantum leap? I wondered. I mumbled, "Lemon chicken." It seemed like an eternity before the waiter brought the food… and then more food and more food. Was I catering someone's party? The evening began to be a blur because I was so livid! He ordered enough food to eat for a month! After dinner, the waiter wrapped up all the extra food to go, and the idiot took my leftovers as well with out even asking if I wanted them. We finally left with two huge doggie bags, which he placed in the back seat.

"I'll drive my own car"," I said as I snatched the keys from the valet. The drive to drop him off was unbearable. Against my better judgment, I just watched him retrieve his two bags of food and then squealed the wheels and burned rubber out of there. I suspect it wasn't his birthday, and he didn't even have a job.

Judy in Long Beach, California

Cyber space is a great buffer zone often allowing people to be more open with each other. With that being said, it also allows anonymity and illusions. Meeting for a coffee or cocktail for a first meeting is a good practice. If chemistry is zero and their pictures are 10 years old you can minimize the "stuck factor" and escape, without it being at your expense!

CHAPTER 4

CYBER NECKING
COLLEGE KIDS

For some reason, There's been a misconception that online dating is for older people who are looking for a second or third marriage, introverts, sociophobes, or professionals who are just too busy to find dates in the traditional way. If this is how you think, think again! With nearly 100 percent of college students glued to their computers 24/7, Generation Y are just as much part of the online dating scene. After all, this Generation craves instant gratification and the ability to connect with the world at their fingertips. The dot.com generation are no strangers to finding love online. According to collegeclub.com, in a survey of 6,700 college aged men and women, 59 percent had met someone from online that they tagged as "great" or "decent." EHarmony has lowered their minimum age from twenty-one to eighteen, realizing the market trend and trying to capture it. There are several other social networking sites that gear themselves specifically at college aged individuals, some of the most popular being Facebook, Twitter, and MySpace. Hold on to your hats, mom! Your kids are dabbling in the cyber world with a vengeance, just like the single parents out there. The only difference is the older generation is looking for a lifelong partner and commitment, while the younger set are looking to meet new people and just have a great time! If you don't want your kids to be playing the virtual field and sowing their cyber oats, my advice to all you parents out there is to lock your kids up and send them to a wire-free convent in Austria! Where are you, Sister Maria?

Note: We have decided to leave out College names and locations due to privacy issues.

THE POETIC GENTLEMEN OR THE FRAT BOY JOCK?

I started online dating and signing up for college networks due to the fact that I was always busy with an internship, my job on the side, and tons of midterms that popped up every now and then. I never really fit in at the college parties because they were all genre filled. There were the punks that went to raves, the vain jocks who had beer pong parties, the goths who would sit around and have movie nights, the indie rockers that would sit around and play music in the dorms, the nerds that studied in the quads, and the super seniors that were complete and utter party animals. Don't get me wrong; the college campus does have a lot of advantages. However, I wanted to meet someone that wasn't attending a bar or party, someone who wasn't surrounded by constant drama in friendship groups.

The one thing I learned about my college experiences is that if you most likely date someone from your college campus, the relationship is soon filled with drama, partying, drugs, and alcohol. I just needed a change. Therefore, I started online dating, endured a few dates with some nice gentlemen, a drug addict, a teacher's assistant (TA), a college graduate, and a few college students from other campuses. Each prospective date was interesting, and I got a bit of diverse experiences while going on dates with the many suitors.

I finally stumbled across a bright-eyed and handsome hunk named Ted. He emailed me, explaining that he wanted to get out of the campus atmosphere and meet someone who was interested in doing the same. "College is such a close-knit community. I have noticed while being in the dorms that a lot of young adults turn to partying instead of focusing on studies," he said.

"I definitely agree. I feel a bit suffocated, so I have tried reaching out through an online dating site to find someone that agrees with me."

I looked at his profile, which showed he was a football player but loved poetry and wanted to try new things. I decided I didn't want to stereotype him as a jock, and we began talking on the phone. He asked me to meet him for coffee in between our colleges, and I eagerly agreed.

As I entered the college oriented coffee shop, I saw many other students sipping coffee with their eyes glued to their laptops, typing away. I saw Ted waving his hand with a huge smile and big burly arms. As I walked over, he gave me a huge hug, and we immediately sat down. We chatted about pop culture, art, poetry, philosophy, professors, international business, music, and other typical college topics. I looked down with a shock at my watch and realized that I was going to be late for my literature class. I bid him goodbye and agreed to go to a frat party at his college the following weekend.

The weekend arrived before I knew it, and I decided to bring a bunch of girlfriends with me to the frat party that Ted had invited me to. I got there a tad bit late and noticed the frat house was humongous, swarming with drunk people left and right. They were having a Mardi Gras party. All the guys sported a ton of beaded necklaces around their necks and explained that the intention of the game tonight is that the girl at the end of the night that gained the most necklaces would win a prize. However, they would have to do something outrageous to gain a necklace. (Like flash their boobs or go streaking across the lawn) I called Ted's cell, and we somehow found one another. We exchanged greetings and introductions with each other's friends, and he handed us a few cocktails. I sat by Ted, and we played a few drinking games like 'Never Have I Ever', 'Circle of Death', and a few others. Ted had great composure, and he was a sweet gentleman all throughout the night. By one a.m, a whooping $5.00 prize was given to the most outrageous girl with the most beads. I bid Ted goodbye, and we agreed to go to the movies the following night.

The following day was a dream come true. This big burly football player gave me a bouquet of roses, and drove us to see a chick flick. Once the movie was over, we went for soup next door, and while we sat down, he confessed that he really adored me and wanted to be in a real relationship. "I like that we can go to parties but also get involved in other things outside of the campus life. I feel like you made a huge step in getting a little involved in my university activities, so I appreciate you dearly. You are bright, beautiful, and open-minded."

I smiled and said, "Yes, I would love for you to be my boyfriend." We have been inseparable ever sense.

Cammie, Nineteen Years Old

THE GOTHIC NYMPOMANIAC

As always, every year I reconnect with newbies that are entering the university world and don't know a soul. Every guy, including super seniors (seniors in their fifth year), considers freshmen a piece of fresh meat. I found that quite repulsive, but I did concur that meeting new freshmen was a great way to make new friends outside of the old friends. I surfed through the Facebook network and noticed that there were a lot of new profiles that suddenly appeared during the summer and the beginning of the fall semester. Freshmen are always the type to party the most, get sidetracked more than anyone, and have the highest dropout rate out of any level or status of a college degree.

I was a junior at my university, the head of my fraternity, Delta Sigma Phi. Every frat boy has a nickname given to him by his frat brothers, and my nickname was Cheese, a nickname that somehow just stuck during my freshman year of rushing. While surfing through Facebook repeatedly like every other college sucker at my university, I came across this beautiful chick who was indeed a freshmen.

This young freshman was from Costa Rica. We will call her Lola. I thought, Wow! An exchange student who probably won't know a soul and won't really be able to communicate very well due to the language barrier. My meal ticket for sure! I noticed her walking to class, hanging out in the quad, playing Frisbee by one of the university buildings, and attending all the parties. She was at the Foam Party, the Pimps and Hoes Party, The Gettin' Laid Party, and the Mardi Gras Party—many of the parties I was forced to host due to being the head of one of the fraternities. I tried to get to know her by offering her alcohol, which isn't the best way of getting to know a girl. However, she somehow showed a keen interest in me, and we began to become close friends. I went to her dorm every day. We chatted about cultures, history, parties, and many other topics.

I noticed that Lola had a hard time speaking English and was very shy, but that didn't matter to me. She was beautiful with her dark black hair and dressed in unusual attire that I found to be very sexy and daring. I also noticed that she fit the genre of being a bit gothic. She loved strange things like dying roses and movies like Edward Scissorhands and The Nightmare Before Christmas. However, I didn't care that we were both different and in opposite social circles. I instantly fell head over heels for her. We began flirting, which turned into a relationship. Things between us became extremely sexual, and we couldn't keep our hands off each other—in the bathroom, on top of a washing machine, in her dorm with no privacy, or somewhere hidden in the quad.

The truth is, I was a virgin until I met her, but she had past experience. We dated for about six months, had a beautiful relationship, and then suddenly she said something really shocking, dropping the proverbial bomb on me. While having sex, she exclaimed, "I think you should have sex with another girl so that you can get more experience." I thought, what the hell? Isn't this a monogamous relationship? My ego and manhood was a bit fractured at this point.

Luckily, Christmas break came, she went back to Costa Rica, and we were able to talk for hours on the phone. I couldn't wait to have her back in my arms, despite the shocking assertion she threw at me before she left.

As soon as she came back, like all college students, we began the decadent and debauchery act of partying every single night.

Since students had been away from the campus and with their families, they were dying to get a fresh breath of air from the university life once again, and this did not include sitting in a library studying. The two of us attended frat parties, beer pong, DJ parties in the quad, and literally got hammered. We also participated in a lot of bong ripping in our friends' dormitories, our safe haven.

AGAIN, Lola dropped another bombshell! While we were arguing, she told me that she had cheated on me with multiple people—someone in Costa Rica, a frat brother, a gay guy, and many other men. What was with this woman? I couldn't believe it. As it turns out, she wanted me to cheat on her because she was cheating on me. I had to have time to think. I did love this Costa Rican girl very much but couldn't believe she would do such a hurtful thing to me. Our relationship had grown so much since we had first met. She had met my family and even my grandmother. My grandmother had given her favorite quilt to Lola as a blessing for our relationship. Was this relationship salvageable?

During the study period, we hadn't seen each other for a couple of days, and I wondered what she had been up to. I tracked her down at a dorm party and saw her there cuddling in the corner with a guy that looked like a short, chubby, rock-star type. I didn't like what I saw. They looked heated and began to make out. My heart was crushed, and I couldn't believe she just stomped on my heart like that. That night, while I was sitting on the balcony upset, the rock-star guy came out wearing my grandmother's quilt naked with Lola there. I began my days of being pissed off at the world and even wanted to drop out of college. I wanted to hurt this guy that stole my girl with every inch of muscle and breath that I had.

The following year, I got through the storm and recovered feeling 100 percent whole again. I began to smile for the first time in months and started participating in activities around the college. I developed closer relationships with my frat brothers once again and started doing much better in my university classes. People kept telling me it was a new year and that I should focus on the new people that had entered the university. Ironically, I did meet another Costa Rican freshman that year. She became my girlfriend, my best friend, and the love of my life. We are still together to this very day!

Cheese, Twenty-Two Years Old

This is a great example of how we do not always understand the purpose of our dating until a later point in time. If it wasn't for "Cheese's" sex-starved siren, maybe he would not have appreciated the girl that came after her. Sometimes we have to kiss (hump) a lot of frogs (however "rabbits" seem more appropriate in her case) before we meet our prince(ss).

THE COLLEGE SLOB

I had moved back into the dorms, and like every other Facebook junkie, I had checked the college networking to see all the new faces and arrivals. Since all college kids get on Facebook chat with all the newcomers, I had started chatting with one of the new fellows on campus. He seemed intriguing, and I was definitely looking for a new and challenging friend! We will call this guy Ehbin. Our first meeting was in the elevator, where I caught him chatting up two very good friends of mine, "college crashers" from England. They actually did not go to the university, but managed to sleep in random dorms and go to the university parties. I had my motorcycle helmet and was carrying boxes and moving furniture, and he immediately took interest in me when he noticed I like to ride motorcycles. He began helping me move my things into my dorm. We chatted about street bikes, books, mixed-martial arts, and other things. He then proceeded to pull up his Ed Hardy t-shirt (great brand) and show me a twelve-inch vertical scar down his entire stomach. He told me a suicider had smashed into his car and that he was rushed into the hospital, where he had actually died on the operating table twice. He began telling me about his endeavors about winning a lawsuit against this woman and his goal of becoming a doctor due to the accident. This guy was a sharp young man with a plan.

He was very good-looking, tall, strong, broad shouldered, 6'2", and fit. He had great style and a bad boy demeanor, not to mention a great wardrobe. He was constantly cursing, throwing out f-bombs every other word. For some reason, I felt like he had a vocabulary in which he could string a hundred curse words together and make it actually sound intelligent with a rugged sensibility. He also drove a sexy car and offered to drop me off at my job on a whim.

At first, I was interested in hanging out with Ehbin but had to focus on my studies and preferred not to go out to clubs like Café Opera or The Velvet Room, join in on paying for a limo, get all dressed up, and spend $100 a night on drinks and cover charges. He kept urging me to come out with him and all the new students, but I stood my ground. One night, one of my roommates began a long, drawn-out romance with one of the three Oxford kids that still exists today. This young man (whom we will call Johnny Cash) stayed in our loft dormitory every night with my roommate and played music and constantly walked in and out of the room naked. Ehbin heard that my current relationship status had changed, probably due to Facebook. He began to come over regularly, bringing new movies like Budge and Trainspotting for us to watch, as well as new books for us to read together. He bought beer like Guinness and Purple Haze for our group of friends, apparently trying to seduce me with his knowledge of culture and alcoholic beverages.

Thanksgiving break we had dinner with my parents, and the next day headed out with friends to Florida. The trip was induced with prescription medication, alcohol, and marijuana—along with a bit of schoolwork, of course. He came up with a brilliant idea to grab a backpack that had a sipping tube for hikers and add beer into it. That way, nobody on the beach saw that we had been drinking beer or chardonnay. After all, we were underage, except for a few of our friends.

We all five of us shared a hotel room and engaged in a buffet of alcoholic beverages, a definite aphrodisiac. He spilled the beans about how much he cared about me. He told me the trip was all about me and that he wanted to seduce me into a relationship. So, I agreed to be his girlfriend. He was such a sweetheart that he even packed my bags the night before the drive home AND drove all the way back inconveniently at three in the morning in order for me to get back for a test I had that following morning. This guy was a keeper!

Our relationship started progressing, and I started noticing he had been slowly moving his things into my dormitory. First it was his clothes, then his books, laptop, underwear, toothbrush, posters, movies, and so on. We even slept together in a twin-sized bed! This started to get annoying, so I sought advice from my roommates. "What should I do? I mean, I can't freakin' sleep at night." We decided this guy had to either get a queen sized futon or get a bigger bed for my dorm if he wanted to cuddle next to me at night. So, we basically had two Oxford boys living with us in this tiny little loft dormitory, even though they had their own dorms for men. And of course, there was drama... Bickering ensued about men leaving their underwear on the floor of the kitchen to women putting tampons in the trash. One of my roommates even started sleeping in a tent in the common area because she became so pissed off at the boys.

Second semester rolled around, and everyone seemed to split up and find other roommates, although we were all still friends. I decided that I needed to focus on my book and got a loft with my Sri Lankan friend, who seemed to be on top of his game as far as studies. Ehbin followed me and moved in all of his stuff as well, even though he had his own dorm. Things started to unravel, and I began to notice all of Ehbin's flaws. He constantly chewed with his mouth open, farted, belched, scratched his butt, let his pants droop low enough to show his butt crack, and slept at least fifteen hours a day. He was also a chain smoker, and he never really took showers. He always peed all over the seat and his feet STUNK so bad that I could smell the reek when I walked in the door. It also appeared that he never ever cut his toenails, and they seemed riddled with fungus. How had I not noticed this? I always tried to suggest that he clean up a bit and that we must compromise for this relationship to work. It got to the point where I started sleeping on the couch because he would make this horrible squeaking and snoring noises while sleeping and randomly kicks me in my sleep. He even cried profusely during Marley & Me! He wept so hard that people had to tell him to be quiet during the movie. What had happened to this guy's man-hood? This man that was once Mr. Sexy and Suave became someone I couldn't even kiss anymore. The lights were out in the romance department. He became Mr. Slob to me, and that turned the lights out right there!

Then, to top that off, he started turning into a hypochondriac. He thought he had Alzheimer's, hyperthyroidism, hyper insomnia, narcolepsy, sleep apnea, ADHD, and everything else. It even got to the point where he speculated that he had ten tumors in his brain. He sat and made doctors' appointments left and right, staring for hours at brain scans. Even after hearing doctors tell him that he was healthy and normal, he would still believe he had all these problems. I tried to be supportive, but I felt this was getting way out of hand. My friends kept telling me that it was just a scam to get more money in another lawsuit. He began running to psychiatrists to get all sorts of medications like Vyvanse, Adderall, Vicodin, Valium, and any pills that could be easily obtained. No wonder he would sleep all day! It got to the point where he had 10 different bottles for different things. He would then tell me that we had to have sex only from three to four in the morning because the pills would not let him get it up any other time. I refused! To top it off, he never left the dorm and became a recluse. At one point, he decided to go for a bunch of brain sleep studies, and they attached a machine on his head with all these freaking wires coming out of his head. He looked like some kind of deranged Bob Marley with electrical dreadlocks. Apparently, it was supposed to monitor his brain waves and activity. He came into my parents' house with this box of wires on his head, and my poor mother, wine in hand, didn't recognize him and started to scream at the Frankenstein-esque intruder.

Somehow, everyone in the dorm had gotten sick with a cold, so I decided to leave the dormitory and stay with my parents for a couple of days. I just had to get away from all the drugs and alcohol. I was kind enough to bring pancakes and food in the morning, which he refused to eat, and I would clean the now filthy disgusting dorm for hours and then leave to go spend the night back at home until the following day. Again, I would enter the dorm with another fresh meal and cough syrup, only to find the place trashed! There were about twenty beers thrown all over, as well as dirty boxers and clothes thrown everywhere and a freaking half-eaten hamburger on the floor, dripping ketchup all over my expensive rug. My disgusting boyfriend was passed out on the couch. I asked him politely, "What happened in here?"

"I effing drank a s—* ton last night with a friend. Can you close the f—* door? I am trying to sleep!" While saying such disparaging statements, he was also scratching at the crotch of the dirty pajamas he hadn't washed in ages. It was absolutely disgusting. At two o'clock that afternoon, I returned to the dorm. When he rolled over and I caught a glimpse of his butt crack protruding out of his pajama pants, I decided I was never ever going to date a slob like that again. I put my foot down, for I had had ENOUGH.

"You do not pay for this dorm," I said. "You still have your own dorm down the hall, and I want you off my couch right this instant. Get the out of my dorm. I want you out!" He got up, shot out a string of a hundred curses at me, and headed to MY bedroom to pass out. Had I not made myself clear? I walked in that room with a strong stride, with complete confidence, and tried to fill my voice with a sense of clarity. "I do not want to date you, and I want you out of my bedroom right this instant." He still wouldn't leave!

I started yelling this time. "I WANT YOU OUT OF MY ROOM OR I WILL CALL SECURITY RIGHT NOW."

Finally, he got up, started screaming back, and began to leave my dormitory while I packed up all of his crap. He then began to beat profusely on my door and woke up my roommate and the entire hallway of dormitories. I refused to let him in, but he stood there for hours, just down the hall from his own dorm. I neatly packed up all of his things one by one, and carefully placed everything outside in the hallway. I refused to ever see him again and called my mother over for support. The guy banged on my door for days, calling me all sorts of names. "Whore! Tramp! I hate you!" He spoke tirelessly to all my friends, spreading rumors about how I had apparently cheated on him, which I had not. Thank God my friends were supportive on my side, even his Oxford buddies! He then sent me a string of text messages telling me he loved me, called me obsessively, ran after me on campus grounds, and even stalked me at a party trying to give me a book of poems he had written for me and pictures of us. He had gone so far as to self-publish it! I was appalled and creeped out, to say the least, and it got to a point where I had to have friends tell him to stop stalking me. He finally got the clue... thank God! Goodbye, Mr. Slob!

Claire, Twenty Years Old

Somewhere in the world there is a dumpster missing its "pig-pen." This is one of the few stories I have read where the person's smell seeped right up through the pages and burnt my nostril hairs. How Claire actually lived with this disheveled dorm rat is beyond my realm of comprehension.

It never fails to amaze me, that while women are laser zapping their faces, injecting the world's most poisonous toxin (Botox) into their faces, and stripping off hair in their most delicate places with piping hot wax—there are still men out there who can't even find the time to throw their boxers in the wash or apply a little Lamisil to their toe nails.

CUTE COUPLE IN COLLEGE

I was in high school and had just gotten out of a very abusive relationship with a guy who had been hooked on cocaine. I was very depressed, wrote poetry all the time, and didn't even know what college I wanted to go to. However, this guy on MySpace started chatting with me. I wasn't interested at first because I was still recovering from the last downfall. He had told me about his college stories, about the brutality of rushing, how he had a girlfriend for a year who cheated on him, and how he had been depressed and decided to drop out of college. He wanted to take some time off and then go back to a different college. I thought he seemed a lot like me, so I decided to meet him. The thing is, we were completely opposite racially speaking. I am Irish American, and he is Indian American.

However, I fell head over heels for him. He turned out to be amazing! He is sweet, docile, committed to his family, and handsome. The only thing that was hard for me was that he is a hyper-insomniac. He stays up for days and sleeps some days fifteen hours a day. When I am with him and spend the night with him, it can be hard to wake him up. Sometimes I have to slap him over and over and then he FINALLY wakes up. Even though he may have flaws, I still love him unconditionally.

We decided to both go to colleges nearby one another and see each other two days during the week and always on the weekends. He became my knight in shining armor! Although, we did go to some wild and crazy parties (we saw a lot of drugs, a lot of sex, and a lot of drunks), we never cheated or hurt one another and never really participated in any of the madness as much as other college students. Maybe I would have participated in everything college had to offer if I had not met Aroon, but he saved me from the mess of being single and alone in a crazy college environment.

Yeah, he was there taking care of me when I was smashed on my twenty-first birthday, and I was there taking care of him when he got drunk one time at a Halloween party, but we never got mad at each other. We never overcompensated with drugs or alcohol. We just wanted to be together and away from all the drama that college has to offer. We have been together for four years now, and we are still in college! We are both working toward our masters' degrees. One day, we will get married and have some beautiful American-Irish-Indian children!

Betsy, Twenty-one Years Old

CHAPTER 5

DISASTER DATES FROM HELL

*"Don't look at the bankbook or the title. Look at the heart.
Look at the soul."*

—First Lady Michelle Obama

Dating is often a pleasurable torture mixed with our imaginable expectations, especially when it is a first-time meeting. More than looks, personality, sense of humor, intelligence, or orientation of your pet turtle, CHEMISTRY is the perennial mystery—stronger even than attraction (although attraction is a big part of the equation) and unrelated to compatibility. If there is truly someone—a scientist, psychologist, priest, or even Dr. Phil who could give us a formula for that powerful little riddle that hijacks and hypnotizes our brains, it would be worthy of the Nobel Prize. We are never sure why it hits, but when it does, we know it! Men usually fall slave to this beguiling force more than women. If chemistry is missing, there is only a limited time before eminent disaster rears its ugly head. Ladies, beware! Men sometimes stick around just for the sex (no kidding!). If there is chemistry, you will find it in the patience of your partner, especially when you can sometimes be demanding or difficult. If they are still smitten, there is something there! If the sparks aren't there, don't waste your time. Settling for less would be the worst kind of missed connection. Forge ahead because at some point, you will be able to look back and chuckle.

A LITTLE JIGGLE IN THE WIGGLE

You know finding a good man is like nailing Jell-O to a tree. We all use what we've got, right? I even had a friend whose potential date sent her a YouTube video of himself in a tight unitard dancing to Beyonce's "If You Like It, Then You Better put a Ring on It." And if you ask me, I think he slipped a big baked potato in the bottom of his unitard. I belong to a number of dating sites. I wasn't desperate; I just thought I would run the numbers and give them all a whirl. A very attractive gentleman by the name of Kevin contacted me through eHarmony. I was taken aback by both his charm and looks, let alone that he was interested in little ole ME!

We had been on two dates, and I was preparing for our third, which was to be a dinner at an Italian restaurant. The outfit I had settled on for the evening included a built-in bra under a flowing blue knit top. I mention the built-in bra because due to my small cup size, I decided to give myself a little more "oompf" by adding silicone inserts. Dinner went great, just as our other dates had; however, on this night, he invited me in for a nightcap. Apparently, he noticed the oompf. The nightcap turned into a mellow make-out session, which generated roving curious hands. I did my best to keep his hands from touching "the girls" and their silicone friends, but it got to a point of becoming laughable. I just decided to let him in on my little secret. "Sweetie, you know I have fake boobs, right?"

He responded, "That's no problem, dear I've known plenty of women with fake breasts. It's okay." Obviously, he had no clue what I was trying to say; he was quite unaware, obviously, that my fake boobs were on the outside. I proceeded again to tell him to which I received the same reply, along with his persistent hands.

At that point, I reached into my shirt and pulled out the insert, which looked a lot like an uncooked chicken breast, and said, "See! They're FAKE!" With his eyeballs bulging and dumbfounded expression, he was at a loss for words. Needless to say, I put my chicken cutlet back in place and drove home, never to hear from the beautiful man again and knowing that I wouldn't be showing up in any eHarmony commercials, oompf or not.

Kristie in Denver, Colorado

Whoa... whoa... whoa there Kristie in Denver! How do you know what he was thinking? You're jumping from A to Z without hanging around to actually find out what this guy might have said. For all we know, he could be sporting hair plugs, a nose job, and was just gathering his thoughts to craft a response. In any event, this story underscores how the ol' bait n' switch can get you into a sticky situation. It's always best to stay as true to yourself as possible.

That being said, we all have our own little tricks of the trade. Maybe we clip in a few hair extensions. Maybe we apply fake lashes to make our eyes pop. Just putting on make-up could be considered a bit of false advertising by some. However, I believe the lesson gleaned here is—we should make sure that by the time we've reached the "making out on the couch" stage, we should be comfortable enough with ourselves to show our true colors, or in Kristie's case—bra size. If it is a deal killer... next!

THE ANTI-SEMITE ALCOHOLIC

Dating is the most delightful uncertainty you'll ever experience. It's like being water boarded by a beautiful girl who's giving you a happy ending at the same time! There seems to be four ways a date can go: super crazy awesome like a Van Morrison song with hot chemistry on a deeper level; respectable you're-not-cuckoo-for-the-Cocoa Puffs, but it was nice, even though there was no strong connection; boring with no sparks whatsoever, nothing in common, and nobody feeling a thing; or finally, A COMPLETE DISASTER SO HORRIBLE AND DEBAUCHED that it is two weeks before you can muster the courage to try again and go on another date.

I was trying speed dating, which is a decent idea on paper but absolutely ineffective in reality. You sit there at a table while X number of women play musical tables and musical men, herded from one table to the next by a five-minute buzzer. Within these five minutes of conversation, you have to surmise if you are interested in dating the person on the other side of the table. At the end of the night, you create a tally of the people you would like to see again and submit it online or to the event leader. In one particular case, I encountered a woman I had once met before at another speed dating event and had not marked as a "yes." She, on the other hand, did mark me as a "yes" this time, so I said to myself, *Why not?*

We decided to go for lunch the next week in Old Town, which was very pleasant. The week after that, we planned to have dinner and hang out at La Jolla Cove. Before we were to meet, she called to inform me that she had had a very difficult week money-wise and wondered if we could just go for drinks. So, we met at TGI Friday's, and I ordered a non-alcoholic beer. She ordered a double martini, which she quickly chugged and said, "Boy, you are going to hate me now" and ordered another martini. I asked for clarification, but she didn't say anything as the conversation continued. My "weirdo" and "lush" sensors were buzzing on vibrate. There were constant references to alcohol. The topic of her two sisters came up. By this time, she was clearly on her way to intoxication. A drunk woman spewing at the mouth is not very attractive, but it is what they spew that is worse than being drunk.

"My sister married an awful man. He's pushy, dominating, and very disrespectful. He is an ARAB!" she said as she downed yet another vodka shot. *This date is going from boring to a disaster,* I thought. By this time, my sensors were on red alert. She was slurring her words a bit and really came out with a doosie that put the "bam" in the date. "I hate the other guy my oldest sister married. He is so opinionated and pushy and cheap. He is so God damn cheap," She rested her third martini on the bar and leaned over to my ear in a hushed tone and said, "He is a JEW," At this point; I was ready to pick up the tab and go. Before I could do so, though, she leaned over and asked with drunken breath, "You're not a JEW, are you?"

"Uh, no, I'm not," I said.

She could not leave well enough alone. "I have nothing against Jews. I mean, they are God's chosen people," she commented.

I couldn't resist. "Well, if you think God chose them to be His people, then why aren't you one of them?" I asked. She was clearly too drunk to process the question, so I promptly waved to the waiter and said, "Check, please,"

As we were walking out the door to head back, she asked, "Do you feel uncomfortable with me driving?"

I really did mind, but I didn't want to insult her, so I asked, "Well, are you okay to drive?"

"Oh, yes. I drive best when I'm drunk anyhow."

I promptly thought to myself *What the f—?* and motioned for a cab. I stuffed her in and sent her home and wondered if I would have better odds at the horse-racing track.

Tim in San Diego, California

Wow Tim, if only you were Mel Gibson, this might have been a match made in_____? Perhaps there is a reason this lady is a frequent speed dater—because if the date lasts longer than seven minutes, she is drunk and slurring her words. This date is a prime example of a deal-breaker. Unless pure unadulterated racism is your bag, you are going nowhere fast. This represents a great example of how important it is to recognize that no amount of second chances, or maybe-she-just-was-nervous thoughts are going to change this person. Clearly there were three red flags; excessive drinking, anti-semitism, and suggesting TGI Fridays for a first date.

MINNOW SHIRT

My friends and I refer to him as "Minnow Shirt," and without hesitation he was bequeathed the honor of a disaster date. I am slightly embarrassed to say Minnow Shirt and I went out a few times before I realized he should have been locked up in the Walmart gun case. On fateful date number five, I remembered to shave my legs, applied extra layers of Rave hairspray (God's gift to flat hair), used deodorant, and sprayed perfume. Then, I awaited Prince Charming. Minnow Shirt arrived twenty minutes late, and when I opened the door to greet him, I am fairly sure my face cringed in the way it would after gulping a cheap tequila shot.

Just so you get the picture, I had carefully selected my trendiest top and a snappy pair of tight fitting jeans. He, on the other hand, was wearing a shirt that your crazy uncle Merv wouldn't wear to the backyard fish fry. It was a neon green button-up with a pattern like some sort of Hawaiian knockoff. You guessed it… there were dorky little minnows all over his shirt! He must have found it at the dollar store, on the 75 percent-off racks, because I don't know anyone who would even pay a buck for it. But I must correct myself here; because he informed me they were NOT minnows. When I asked, "Are those minnows all over your shirt," he arrogantly replied "No. Do they look like a bunch of exactly identical uniform fish?"

I answered, "Uh, yes they do."

"Obviously, you don't like to fish or know anything about fish," he retorted coldly. My fish naiveté then generated a thirty-minute lecture (no kidding) from Minnow Shirt on the distinct differences and variances between all the fish on his shirt. I thought for a moment he was going to take his shirt off and lay it flat as not to miss a single fish. "These are MINATURE sized versions of full sized assorted species of fish—NOT MINNOWS!" *Well, give me a dunce cap for fishing class,* I thought.

Despite my harsh debriefing on the anatomy of fish, for some stupid reason I continued on the date. Dinner and conversation was tense, to say the least. We headed over to the bar for drinks. To my luck, the fish gods were in full force that night. My date plopped his pudgy butt on the stool next to a girl who was wearing a giant fish pendant around her neck—I kid you not! It easily rivaled Flava Flava's plate-sized bling. I almost put on my sunglasses inside to save my eyes from the glare. I was amazed that her neck wasn't tired!

So, the bar's only two fish friends began to strike up a heated conversation delving deeply into fishing, fishing poles, fishing boats, kinds of fish, places to fish, and the best way to cook fish. All the while, Minnow Shirt kept his back turned to me—his real date. He proceeded with his fish companion to make fun of me for my fish ignorance while I aimlessly chewed on my straw and made origami figures out of the bar napkins—needless to say, I didn't bother trying to make an origami fish, fearing a further lecture if I didn't fashion the fins to scale. Minnow Shirt proceeded to get Minnow Pendant's number right in front of me. The fact that I had no interest in fish was obviously a deal breaker. Facebook informed me after that the couple has been having a happy, fishy relationship for six months. If I happen to get an invitation to their wedding, I will be sure to send them a Fry Daddy and wish them luck!

Annie in Pittsburg, Pennsylvania

My question Annie is why on earth did this guy get to the fifth date? I think this is a common mistake a lot of women (and men) make. It's as if it's been so long since we've had a decent date that we don't even recognize when a bad one is right in front of us.

I think it is always a good idea to give a guy (or gal) a second chance, if there were not any blatant deal breakers in the first meeting. Chemistry and compatibility is not always something that pops up on the first date (and if it does it does not always mean this is your soul mate, but rather they remind you of something earlier in your life, which you are now comfortable with).

However, if after date two, we think more about when our mailman is going to come than when we are going to see them again—it is probably not worth wasting anymore of your time. So go on and cut your losses early before they show up wearing the minnow shirt—there are plenty of fish in the sea.

"Men want the same thing from their underwear that they want from women: a little bit of support, and a little bit of freedom."

—Jerry Seinfeld

Tips for Women

Play hard-to-get the right way. A man who is desirous will pursue you. Don't give too much at once! Just leave him wanting more. Give him flirtatious hints without taking your stockings off. Make him work a little for his cookie.

Don't nag or gripe. A big turn-off to a man is a woman who is not satisfied with anything. If the steak is too bloody, go ahead and send it back, but if there aren't enough bubbles in the soda, don't keep bringing it up all night long. If he thinks you will never be happy with anything, he probably thinks he'll never measure up and that you aren't worth the shot to his ego.

Don't let your cell phone detract from the evening. Communicate with your work, your friends, or your children on your own time! If you are on a date, you are sharing time with the man you're with. It's completely rude to be laughing at texts of inside jokes while your date is staring at the ceiling wondering if the jokes are at his expense.

Know about guy things. Brush up on this stuff! It's fun to be able to talk to men about their hobbies—even if it's the latest Xbox game or their favorite baseball team.

Avoid excessive whining. Men are usually brick walls when it comes to complaints (unless they are gay). They may sympathize for a couple of minutes, but don't expect them to feel comfortable being a shoulder to cry on before six months into the relationship! If your mother is a witch, then talk to your girlfriends—your date doesn't want to hear about it, and if you keep mentioning it, he might think you take after your mother.

Be ready to flirt. Believe me, guys need this. It's like helium in a balloon! Men naturally need their egos stroked, so feel free—just don't do too much stroking too soon.

Marriage is a four-letter word (in man-talk). Even the most charming Prince Charming, is generally terrified of you expecting too much commitment and all too soon. It is like nails on a blackboard. He is supposed to propose to you someday, and he knows this already. Look too eager and he'll assume you are looking for some sort of slave. There is a reason men call their wives "the old ball and chain." Wait till he's ready!

Stop jabbering. Know that you have 10,000 words to his every ten. Help him express himself by asking him questions that he'll be happy to answer. You need to do this because you want to get to know who you're getting involved with—and again, it doesn't hurt to flatter him by letting him tell you all about himself.

Hygiene check. Bad breath is a death sentence. Wear sexy perfume that is complimentary to your personality. The hair on your head (not under your arms or on your legs) is like a halo to men. Be sure to keep it clean, as men are sensory animals.

Make love a lot. C'mon girls! Use your imagination and creativity. Your mom was wrong: the way to a man's heart is NOT through his stomach.

THE MOTHER-IN-LAW

One day, I came home to find a few emails in my in-box from match.com. I was shocked to see one from a sixty-one-year-old woman. She was clearly attractive, but my profile stated "woman looking for a man." Out of curiosity, I opened her email to find out she was actually playing matchmaker for her never-married son. She said I was "darling" and would be a good match. He was not online or in a dating service, but if I was interested, she would have him contact me directly and send his photos. This was definitely an unconventional way to meet a man, even in the twenty-first century, but I was intrigued. Mom sold me on all of his great qualities. Since I passed the mother-in-law test, I gave her my email address so her son could contact me directly. The very next day while I was enjoying Bossa Nova night at the Hollywood Bowl with my girlfriends, the ever so shy son sent me an email, along with three photos for us all to examine. I got a group approval and decided to write back. He said he was an investment banker who was almost forty-three but claimed, "I look like I'm in my mid-thirties." He added that he was fit, athletic, easy going, a good cook, and someone who works and plays hard. He said he was tired of the dating scene in the Beverly Hills *area*, where he lived. The area was clearly not all too Beverly Hills.

I was concerned that he had never been married at forty-three, and we all thought it a bit odd that he wore the same blue shirt in all three shots. One girlfriend thought he had nice eyes, and the other said he had nice legs. I wondered if maybe we would be double dating with his mother and one of her match dates. It's a crazy world out there, and almost anything goes these days! I was actually hoping she might come along as a chaperone on our first date.

The next morning, I sent him an email with my phone number so we could graduate to a conversation and make some plans. My intuition (by the way, ladies, we are 99.9 percent correct… ask any detective) somehow made me feel as if there were something Mom had not revealed. There is usually a good reason why a man in his forties still wishes he was in his thirties and has never been married. I typed my potential cyber date's personal email address in Google to search out what kind of investment banker this bachelor was. Words cannot describe the look on my face when I saw his personal ad on the first page of Google. My potential new mother-in-law's son had placed an online ad in a casual encounters group and swingers group, and I'm not talking about swing dancing! *Man*

Seeking Woman Tantra Partner in Los Angeles, read the ad. His poor mother was out there trying to find her little angel a wife, and only a month earlier, the sleaze had posted this ad online. He claimed to be in his thirties and said he was searching for "X-rated women," and he certainly did not appear marriage minded. He wanted women to email him their fantasies and desires and claimed he was an expert in "G-spot massage." I don't think Mom knew about her darling boy's extracurricular activities, but ladies, follow your intuition... and don't forget to Google, Google, Google!

Julie Spira in Los Angeles, California (excerpt from *The Perils of Cyber-Dating: Confessions of a Hopeful Romantic Looking for Love Online*)

> *Tantras, and G-spots, and mothers oh my! What a great use of Google Julie. It seems your intuition was right on when questioning why a forty-something man who is marriage-minded, yet never been married is being set up by his mother. Your keen dating prowess guided you to Google him before you wasted 1 hour talking on the phone, 1.5 hours getting ready, 2.5 hours pretending to be interested as he used words like "sensual," "princess," and started sentences off with "you know I'm a very physical person." You did lose out on the expert G-spot massage, but you also gained five hours of your life back.*

"Men want a good looking, sex starved slaved chef who owns a liquor store; women want a man who compliments, comforts, spends money on them, is supportive, attentive, loves and adores them, and would go to the ends of the earth for them."

—Jeff Foxworthy

Tips for Men

Bathe. Women are the cleaner species and are more apt to be bothered by the grit and grime on their partners. After all, you wouldn't live with a scrounged mutt taken from an alleyway for a day. C'mon, Grizzly Adams, clean yourself up for the ladies!

Be on time. If you're running late, guys, give her a heads up. Women are prone to exaggerating things in their heads and taking them the wrong way entirely. Even if you have a flat tire on the way, have to follow a funeral procession, or the dog ate one of your shoes, she will immediately think you are late because you don't care about her unless you call her to let her know why.

Bring a thoughtful gift. Notice the key word here is thoughtful, not necessarily pricey. The fact is that you should be paying attention to her likes and dislikes, and a perfect way to show her you've been listening is to bring her something she likes. Remember, all women love flowers!

Be a gentleman. Opening the door, pulling out her chair at the table, picking up the bill, and walking beside not ahead of her might seem like old-fashioned hullabaloo, but these little shows of attention will guarantee that you have hers.

Compliment her. Like all human beings (yes, men, believe it or not, women ARE human) women love to be complimented and to feel special. They should feel beautiful and attractive to you. If not, it puts in question why you're with her. "If you want a poke, then you better stroke'

Listen well. This tip should be a no-brainer by now. Think of it as studying for a test, and if you get a gold star on this test, it is something you'll truly enjoy.

Flip for the bill. As much as women like to feel they have girl power, they also like to be taken care of. Chivalry is not dead. Pick up the tab for dinner, but if your modern-day girl power Cinderella insists on going Dutch, don't insult her by insisting that you pay.

Keep it hot and heavy. Be extremely attentive in this area! Check out her body language and be aware of signals she is giving off. The first kiss may boost the chemistry between you to the moon, or might be considered to aggressive. Check the signals guys!

Learn to carry on a conversation. Umm is not the word when it comes to impressing a female date. Be attentive and animated when you are talking. Don't be a bore, for no one wants to be stared at or lectured. Play the game well... don't lie, listen well, and be charming.

To call or not to call. Never say you plan on calling if you are not interested in pursuing her. If you really like her, call when you say you will, but if you don't then do not start to create a tangle of hurtful lies and crushed hopes. Confusing a woman is dangerous business and quite possibly harmful.

INEPT MR. HARVARD

I was drinking my coffee and checking emails, my usual routine, when I noticed a handsome face on my screen from match.com. His profile said "Graduate of Harvard Business School and Retiring McKenzie Consulting Partner." *Hmm... a man with a big bulge—and in his back pocket, which doesn't hurt!* Some things might just taste better rich, like chocolate, coffee, beef bourguignon, and men. I thought that forty-eight was awful young to be retiring, but everyone lies about their age online, right? I know I did, so who was I to judge? We met, and I found him fascinating with impeccable credentials. He told me he never went to a party in college because all he did was study, and he graduated *Magnum Cum Laude*. I told him that all I ever did in college was party and I barley graduated. We had a lot in common—NOT! I had never dated anyone so brilliant and smart. It was a little intimidating. We dated for a few months. Once, he gave me a report he had published in the *Harvard Business Review*. He told me to read it so we would have something to discuss. It was the business matrix model of a Fortune 500 company—not exactly some Fabio-covered easy reading Harlequin paperback. It was all I could do to hold back the laughter because he was dead serious about having "something to discuss." I thought, *Okay... socially introverted nerd meets fun loving gregarious big haired ex beauty queen.* You guessed it! We would have never dated in high school. He was really handsome and such a genius, but he always said the wrong things and had no sense of humor. For every ounce of book smarts he had, he lost an ounce of social charisma. And the fact that he did not drink any alcohol didn't help. Unfortunately, he was not a foodie and pizza was high on his list. As a matter of fact, on one of our dates at a pizza joint I mentioned that I needed to bring a pizza home to my kids for dinner. After dinner, I also mentioned I left my purse in his car. "I'll go out and get your purse," he said. What odd behavior for a man who bragged about making $1,000,000 a year and drove a $70,000 car! *Get my purse? What about pulling out that wallet of yours, Mr. Harvard man!*

I actually mentioned that I thought it was cheap of him, and in response, I received a thirty-minute analytical lecture of why it was not his responsibility to pay for his girlfriend's kids' dinner. I paid the $12 and took the pizza home. He was a complete genius with no common sense. He just could not understand why he didn't get any that night, but sometimes you get what you give.

We continued to date, trying to fit a square peg into a round hole, so to speak. The mother of all intellectual flubbers came as we were making love when he wanted to solve math problems in the middle of trying to get me to reach an orgasm. "Oh, baby the square root of 38 is OOOOHHHH!" Should I scream or should I laugh? Actually, I didn't know the answer, so I just screamed and moaned. Hell, I needed a calculator in bed with this man!

Our final date ended when I went to Florida to his home before it sold due to the divorce. We had a wonderful dinner in Key West, and I had put on a sexy nightie. "I'll be right up," he said. "I just need to check my business emails," In spite of our previous difficult equation, there I was all dressed ready to give him a happy ending. Finally, I went to check on him, only to discover that the "business emails" he was looking at were from match.com. To say the least, there was definitely a hurricane swarming in that household that evening. There was no intellectual reasoning (which the devil couldn't beat him at), nothing analytical, nor even a bold-faced lie that would have salvaged that relationship after that. I promptly took the guest bedroom and flew home the next morning. It was a disaster I should have seen coming. After all, good sex should never involve solving for a problem!

Lisa in Atlanta, Georgia

Ahh, the 'looks good on paper' guy. This guy is so tempting to many of us women and I blame it all on

Clark Kent with his befuddled looks and his knowing blue eyes peering out of those nerdy little spectacles. The problem is that while intelligence is a turn-on—we really want Superman. Deep down we want a man that is going to throw us over their back, fly us to their cave… er home, and tear off our clothing. Not someone who is pontificating the square root of pi. They usually say God giveth with one hand and taketh with the other, and the case is certainly true for this bloke. Like the pretty girl who never had to develop a personality, it goes to show we should never judge a book by its cover—even if it's from Hahhh-vahhhd.

THE TRAGEDY

"Looking for a best friend who will share dessert," was the headline that drew me into contacting Vickie. After exchanging a few icebreakers over the phone, we agreed to meet for a cocktail after work. I felt 80 percent sure her picture was authentic, but the other 20 relied on prayers alone. When she showed up, I realized the prayers worked. She looked absolutely fantastic. She was a blue-eyed blonde with an adorable little figure. After so many disappointments with online meetings, this was a pleasant surprise.

She had recently gone through a divorce after many years of marriage. Looking for an apartment with damaged credit and not much money in a down economy is not an easy thing for a single mom with a teenage son. I thought she was such a sweetheart that I just had to help her out. I put her in touch with a friend who managed an apartment complex in the area, and she bypassed the credit checks. Vickie also mentioned that she had just started a new job at a passport agency. That was great to know because mine was about to expire, and I had to leave for London on business. She took care of everything and expedited my passport for me. Her sweetness endeared her even more. Luckily, the passport came the day I was to leave, and she rushed over to hand-deliver it to my office.

"Have a great trip! Call me when you get back."

"Definitely," I said as I gathered up my briefcase to rush out the door. I really liked her and felt an immediate connection.

After landing back in Atlanta, I made a surprise visit to her office with some Scottish shortbread cookies. She had such a look of appreciation and seemed delighted to see me. "Would you like to go to a hockey game this Friday?" I asked, wondering if someone hadn't snatched her up already.

"Absolutely," she said, giving me a big warm hug.

We had a fabulous time at the game, but as I was driving up to her office where I had picked her up, she had a peculiar request. She asked that I not drop her off at her car but across the street at the parking deck about a hundred feet away. "Is there something wrong? Is someone following you?" I asked.

"No. He knows it's over, but I am just always cautious," she said as she closed my door, disappearing in the dim light. I had a strange feeling but thought, *In for a penny, in for a pound.* I asked her out again for the next week.

We agreed to meet at the bar at eight p.m., and she showed up promptly at eight forty-five without so much as a call—another red flag I should not have ignored. She apologized but seemed frazzled and totally distracted from any conversation we were having. Her son called, and she proceeded to have a twenty-minute conversation with him in the middle of dinner. Red flag number three. "Is everything okay with you?" I asked.

"Oh, yes. I'm sorry for the interruption, but there are just a lot of changes going on, and my son is taking it very hard," she said. I decided then and there that she had too much baggage, and I didn't feel like carrying it. The timing wasn't right, so I decided that after our date, I would not pursue her further.

After several weeks went by, I got a call while working in New Orleans. It was Vickie. It was great to hear her soft voice. "Hey, you have been so kind to help me with getting an apartment. I'm moved in, and I would love to cook dinner for you and have you over." It was a sweet gesture, and I did want to see her again, hoping things had calmed down for her. The next Saturday, she called me that morning with excuses about her house being in disarray.

"That's fine. We can just eat out instead," I offered.

We had a great dinner, and she insisted on paying for it, which I knew she couldn't afford. I took care of the bill in spite of her offer, and we went back to my place and played some "couch games" for a few hours before I dropped her off at home.

The next date was another forty-five-minute late arrival and another twenty-minute phone conversation with her son about her ex-husband. By this time, the red flags were waving like mayday in Moscow, and I decided it was all too much drama for me, a relatively undramatic kind of guy.

My phone rang several weeks after that date, and I had not seen Vickie since. Terri, my apartment manager friend, asked, "Have your heard the news?"

"What news?"

"That woman—that Vickie—was murdered last night! The police called and arrived to a triple homicide.

The tale sent a chill up my spine and haunts me to this day. Apparently, Vickie had a male friend over for dinner when the doorbell rang. Her ex-husband drew a gun and shot Vickie between the eyes, shot her dinner guest, and fatally shot himself. All I could think was *It could have been me!*

Looking back, I guess I should have paid more attention to the red flags. I also feel relieved that the dinner guest was not me. But beyond all of that, I have a profound sorrow for a cute little blonde that didn't deserve such a tragic ending.

Gary in Atlanta, Georgia

This is a horribly unfortunate tragic side of dating. This circumstance is more common than you think, and can happen to anyone online or off. It is a prime example of why you should be cautious about dating someone separated or newly divorced. You never know the emotional fragility or instability of an ex partner. The risks and red flags were presented blatantly through the fear of being dropped off away from a vehicle and the chaotic drama ensuing with each date. Clearly there needed to be more distance at the time. Be aware of your circumstances with others to protect yourself. Pay attention to your gut feeling and go with it!

CHAPTER 6

ONLINE FRENZY OF LOVE OR LUST?

"When you fish for love, bait with your heart not with your brain."

—Mark Twain

We have come to learn that 75 percent of people online are looking for a long-term relationship. But the question is, in the virtual world how do we know what is *real* or when its time to move on? What are the signs that we are dating the right one? We must be able to communicate well beyond emails and pillow talk, and knowing someone before we commit takes time. There are some good signs you might be heading in the right direction for instance being open and honest about your feelings with one another, and not hesitating to express them freely to the person you are with, as well as to friends. "Baby you're so hot I am going to explode" is most certainly a compliment in its own right, but wouldn't it sometimes be just as nice (or nicer) to hear, "You are incredibly special, and I care a lot about you," expressing a real and wonderful connection? If you are not hearing this within six months of dating then you are still a character of the virtual online reality show. If a meaningful relationship is what you want you might consider returning to the man menu.

Hints you could be in love: You can argue together but can always compromise to find a solution that satisfies both of you, whatever the issue. When you are crazy about somebody, you WILL work it out because it's not just lust but love as well. When you love someone, you try to do anything to fix a situation or make a suitable compromise. When you fall for someone, you end up talking about substantial life issues like finances, children, things that frighten you, ambitions, and so on. Why? It's because when you are in love with someone and feel they are in love with you, you feel safe being vulnerable with that person.

Love is a wonderful thing, and relationships rarely survive without it. There are signs other than goose bumps that you might just be in love. In a crisis, you stand by each other, no matter what the result. You will make sacrifices to make that person happy and keep no secrets or hold no regrets. You are best friends as well as lovers.

BUT, if you aren't in love, you'll know it. Whether you say it or not, something inside you will warn "Whoops! It's time to call it quits. *Hasta la vista,* baby!" When the going gets tough, you may find your partner emotionally or physically absent with an "I don't want to be bothered" attitude, leaving you to work things out on your own. Maybe your partner has a roving eye, or maybe you can't help feeling like the grass is possibly—no, probably—greener on the other side. There is little physical affection, laughter, or good communication, and maybe that's because your partner is sleeping with someone else—hopefully not your best friend.

When you experience true LOVE, it's ineffable and unexplainable. True love comes when the moderate part of ourselves is interested more in our partners spiritual growth and happiness more than our own. True love is the act of loving someone after we've done our taxes together and after we have seen them read the New York Times on the crapper. If you have ever been in love, you know that there comes a point when you can't resist that person and you can't stop thinking about them. But remember that there are different types of love. The strongest one that keeps people together is a love that is always patient and always kind. It's never a jealous type of love, never boastful, and never conceited. True love is ready to excuse, to trust, to hope, and to endure whatever comes.

Everyone wants to be in love and to stay in love with "the one"—that perfectly right-for-you person that sticks by your side through thick and thin. Smart love is not blind but is aware of the signals to know what is real and what is not. Capturing it is worth the effort.

THE SOFTBALL LOVERS

I met Chris met via eHarmony.com in August of 2005. Chris was coming off a terrible relationship and really just wanted to focus on his career and sports. I had lived in Atlanta for a year and had struggled to meet the "right kind" of guys. Both of us thought it was a long shot but would throw something out there in the online dating community and see if anything came of it. I felt that my friends and family would confirm that dating online would be somewhat uncharacteristic of me, but I had to give it a try. I completed the personality questionnaire and posted profile pictures. eHarmony began sending compatible matches, and less than two weeks later, I was matched with Chris and added him to the list of compatible matches.

Chris was very shy when it comes to girls, so luckily I saw something in his profile that made me initiate contact. I noticed that we both love to play sports and are avid sports fans. I noticed that like me, Chris also played softball during the week and was on several teams. We both were members of LA Fitness, but were members at different locations. Knowing all this, I was doubtful our paths would have ever crossed had it not been for the cyber collision we had through eHarmony.

In Chris's profile, I saw that we had a lot of the same interests, particularly when it came to playing and watching sports. He seemed like he was very excited about his job and seemed very passionate about his career. He made comments about how important his family and friends were to him. Scattered among these tell-all facts about Chris were also some photos. In the picture of him holding a dog, I noticed his outstanding biceps. The information in his profile (not to mention those biceps) peaked my interest and curiosity, so I made the first move to initiate contact. My first step was to choose four multiple-choice questions for Chris to answer. If he wanted to continue, he could read my profile to find the answers, and then respond with four questions of his own.

After Chris received the inquiry from my message, he looked further at my profile and explained to me that I was really the female version of him. Some folks say that opposites attract, and that may be true, but opposites as far as Chris was concerned did not stand the test of time. He needed to be with someone who had a lot in common with him. After he answered the questions that I sent over, he was able to send a few questions of his own as well. He was very pleased with the answers he got back, and it was almost to the point of moving into a series of "can't stand" and "must have" questionnaires. Once again, the answers matched up really well, and before long, Chris explained that he couldn't wait to talk to me.

The next step was open discussion questions. Each had to come up with three open-ended questions, which were exchanged as before. After this, we began to email each other through eHarmony. The back-and-forth emails went on for a few days before we decided to speak on the phone, and he gave me his phone number.

Once I was in the driver's seat again, I decided to call Chris on a Wednesday night, and then we spoke for over two hours about everything imaginable. One of us would throw out a topic, and we would just keep right on talking. The connection was unbelievable. The next night, we spoke again for about the same amount of time and decided to go on our first date that Friday. At this point, I figured I had enough reason to think he wasn't an axe murderer, and I couldn't wait to meet him.

We were both very excited but very nervous. We decided to meet at Nava in Buckhead. He arrived first, and I can still remember walking up and experiencing the nervous anticipation of seeing him for the first time. There he was, in a black shirt and jeans, looking just as nervous as I was feeling on the inside. I wasn't sure whether to greet him with a handshake or a hug. Fortunately, Chris finally took some initiative and gave me a big hug. Being the ever-competitive athlete that he was, he challenged me to a few before-dinner games at the ESPN Zone before dinner.

We continued on to dinner and had a fantastic meal as well as conversation. Afterwards, we went out to a couple bars, and the evening could not have been better. We said goodnight and have been inseparable ever since. We both were each other's first and only online date.

One year and four months later, we got engaged, and on April 12, 2008, we were married. Without eHarmony's methodical compatibility test and taking a chance online, we are not sure we would have ever met. eHarmony allowed us to really get to know each other *before* we ever met face to face. For some people it hasn't worked, and for others it has, but in the case of Chris and me, we agree that it was the best $50 that we ever spent.

Kimi in Atlanta, GA

MR. MAGNUM

I had always dated the traditional way. I ended up getting married like every other good-looking guy who needed to stop playing and start committing. But when the marriage ended in divorce a few years ago, my buddies introduced me to MySpace. I was blown away at how easy it was to "date," the code for getting laid. The dating world had just exploded! I met girls left and right—girls that liked me in an instant. I would go on dates, sometimes with nine different girls a week! Boy, I was in a very lustful mood! It seemed like every woman on MySpace was flirting with me, some of them telling me I look like a mix between Brad Pitt and Robert Redford. I started my sexcapades with HOT women between the ages of eighteen to fifty. Since I work for the Big 4 accounting firm, this did not portray a normal looking life, but I was a BABE MAGNET. My friends nicknamed me MAGNUM because anytime I went anywhere, I had girls chasing me and asking me for my number or outright for SEX. This was all so new to me because I had always lived a cookie-cutter life as a child. I went to a very conservative small college and after graduation just got married to my college sweetheart. But now, things had changed. I started hooking up with playboy bunnies, maxim girls, models, housewives, married women, students, and any other HOT chick that wanted me.

The whole thing was quite unbelievable, really… one fling after another. With one of the girls I met, I was having hot, lustful sex right there in the parking lot within thirty minutes of meeting her! On another occasion when I was in Vegas with my buddies, I decided to meet another girl from Facebook who was there with a bachelorette party since she was such a flirt. Within one hour of talking out on the fire escape, she asked me to f—* her right then and there. When I saw her the next day at the resort with her girlfriends, I thought, "*This is great!*" Then she gave me some shocking news. "I'm engaged. My fiancé is on his way, and we are getting married today," she said. *WOW!* I thought, "*I just had sex with a woman—on a fire escape, no less— one night before she was going to be married!*" What happens in Vegas stays in Vegas!

My bedroom escapades had little to do with bedrooms, really, because I started having sex EVERYWHERE—in the park, in the movie theatre, on top of buildings, on the stairs, in hallways, in the middle of the street, in the ocean, in the hot tub, in a public bathroom, in the middle of dinner underneath a table at a restaurant, and many other crazy places. I really stopped counting how many people I had had sex with, but didn't want to become the new "*Wilt Chamberlain.*" The excitement of the chase is such an addiction. I just love women and can't help it!

These days, I am married, but every once in a while, that lustful side creeps up, and I feel like getting out there in the world of the many hot, beautiful, sexy women and playing the game all over again.

Mike in Atlanta, Georgia

C'EST LA VIE MARCO

I was surfing through match.com and encountered a beautiful French man who showed interest in me. We will call him Marco. The two of us decided to meet instantly, and he swept me clear off my feet. He was so handsome, attentive, romantic, and an artist to boot! We had a weekend of lust and passion on the beach. We read poetry, sang songs, and danced the nights away! We saw each other again for weeks at a time. I was addicted to spending time with him, and he was addicted to me. I always felt that the French language was the language of love, so I melted whenever he spoke French to me. He would say things like, "*Tu as de très beaux yeux*" ("You have beautiful eyes"). We did everything together, from going out surfing, to tango dancing, to wining and dining. Sometimes, while sitting and chatting along the beach, he would say things like, "*Qu'est ce que je ferais sans toi?*" ("What would I do without you?")

We began to have a long, drawn-out relationship. In spite of this closeness, however, he made it clear that he never liked me visiting him at his apartment on the spur of the moment without fair warning, and he definitely did not want me to meet his friends. I started asking questions. "Are you afraid to show me to your friends?"

"No," he would say. "But my friends are just animals. They are players and have been encouraging me not to be in a relationship with you. I want to keep my social life with my buddies and my relationship with you separate. You see... I have fallen in love with you, and my friends aren't taking it so lightly."

I was shocked! *What kind of friends does he have?* I wondered. I decide to do some digging. I followed him and his buddies to a nightclub with a girlfriend of mine, and I couldn't believe what I saw. He was right, because they were animals. They were smacking women's a—*, grabbing their boobs, and taking females back to the apartment where everyone got happily laid. I overheard Marco arguing with his buddies. "Look," he said, "I know we decided to get on match.com just to get laid, but I am getting sick and tired of this bulls—*. I really do love this girl."

The animals responded, "How could you love her? You had so many chicks before you met her. You were a player then, and you still are now. You are too young to get tied down. Look, it's either her or us! We are your buddies and we are all in this together. Women are nothing. It's all about the SEX."

I was mortified. I went straight home and cried myself to sleep. The man I had loved was an imposter. Was it really all about the lust for him? How could I have not seen this before? I had fallen in love with this man, and now I just felt crushed. He had taken something from me, a part of my heart. I felt my heart break into a million pieces! I confronted him the following day, only to find that the end result was that he just wasn't ready for love. He ended up choosing his friends over me and lust over love instead.

Rachael in Los Angeles, California

Not bad enough that you found our old skunk friend, Pepé Le Pew, but you also had to find him in Los Angeles. In the land of 'sticks with tits," it can be difficult to land a man even if you are a rocket scientist that also happens to moonlight as a Victoria's Secret model on the weekends.

This illustrates why it is important to understand that in times of rejection, it is often more about them, than it is about you. When these situations happen, it is important to take inventory of the reasons this person is unavailable. In this case, old frenchy is surrounded by a cluster of LA d-bags that will probably be carrying his oxygen tank for him when he's in his golden years. Thank his friends for saving you from further hurt and forget about the French fry.

SHELTER YOU THROUGH THE STORM

I made the difficult decision to leave the Catholic priesthood to find someone I could fall in love with. I wasn't involved with anybody for twenty years, so this was a huge leap of faith for me. I decided to sign up with match.com, and I was intrigued by the many responses I received. I am forty-five years old but have never been married or had kids. At one point in my life, my loyalty was to the church and only to the church. I decided to embark on a new life once I left the priesthood. Foolishly, I disclosed my past with my first date about my personal history. When I met my first date, a very beautiful and successful woman, I told her my story, and she gave me a bewildered look and said, "Oh, poor you. Would you like to get laid?" The second date was exactly the same. I wondered if there was something wrong with me. I was not looking to get laid; I was just looking for a great relationship. Was it the cologne I was wearing? I was confused beyond belief. I thought, *maybe women are just nurturing and want to show it through intimacy?*

I endured many other dates, explained my story, and received the same response consistently. I ended up getting off match. com for a while and thought about the method of dating. For a long time, I just didn't understand what I was doing wrong because I was being honest with women. I had always thought that in a society as broken and confused as ours, women often suffer because they are misunderstood and expected to be a certain way. It seemed to me that 99 percent of the women I met felt their bodies were defective in a certain way and once they were over forty, they are done.

I decided to get back online but did not mention my priesthood past this time. I saw a profile of a beautiful, seemingly intelligent woman, and I was very fascinated. We corresponded for a while, and when we met, to her merit, she said right away, "Well, I feel the need to tell you about my history. I have two children. One is five and one is three." This woman was very bright, and she carried a Ph.D. She was a put-together person. So, bearing all that in mind, I'll admit I was a bit shocked when she revealed, "My ex is a woman. I received my children from a sperm donor. We had two children, and it didn't work out. We now share joint custody of the children." She then told me that she did not want to be in that kind of relationship anymore and that she wanted to be in a heterosexual relationship with a man. She said it in such a way that she wanted to see my reaction. As a former priest, I am very empathetic to the human condition. I did not judge her.

I appreciated her honesty and told her about my story. I explained to her that I had been a Catholic priest for the last twenty years. I felt that we both had something in common. Women had been all over me, and the probability of men that ran away from her past was possibly innumerable. I told her,

"You have these two beautiful children. It is fantastic to be a mother to them, and I am sure these gorgeous little kids love you!" I ended up falling in love with this woman, despite her past—after all, we all have them! Her honesty wasn't going to turn me away, and through the space between what's wrong and what's right, I ended up loving her more.

Jamie in Atlanta, Georgia

This is such a great example of how love can prevail if we just throw away our list of check boxes. All of those "must be tall," "must be well-traveled," "must be," "should be." If we look at our own reflection, we can probably see many mistakes and regrets we made as a result of simply being human. Next time we meet someone, let us take a lesson from this former priest, let go of our judgments, simply be present, and let our heart lead the way.

LITERATURE LOVE BIRDS

I first used chat rooms with AOL in the early nineties and was intrigued by the phenomenon of being able to integrate into a social circle that saw way beyond physical appearances. In my real life, I was a shy, self-loathing, dateless virgin at twenty-three, but in a chat room, I could be someone else. In the chat room, I could be honest about my desires, my opinions, and my feelings on any issue—I could be ME. As geeky as it may seem, for an introvert like me, this phenomenon was a major help in my self-discovery. Nerdy or not, it became my social circle. However, chatting became a short-lived faze, and I later left the social circle of the chat world.

In 1997, after some very tumultuous years in my wild young adult life, I became a single mom, and I remained that way for nine years, doing not much in my life but living to get back on good terms with my family and church. I chose to cut off my social life completely outside my family and church, and I didn't go on so much as a date in almost ten years. But in 2005, I got bored. Not knowing where else to go to ease myself back into a social life, I wandered back into the chat rooms, this time on Yahoo. I was looking only for friends to connect with and had no plans to pursue anyone romantically, which is why my chat room of choice was "Books and Literature 2" instead of a dating room. I was a writer, and I thought it would be a good place to sell my recently published books and talk to people who like to read.

After I had been chatting in the same room for a couple of months and gotten to know many of the people, a guy came online who seemed so sweet. He went by draft_of_shadows, and I found his chat name intriguing most of all at first. After a while, it became clear that he had a "thing" going on with one of the chatters in the chat room who had since become one of my good friends. I became like a big sister to the two of them because we all three got along well. Through a series of IMs, emails, and phone calls, they both came to me for advice on their relationship, asking me questions like "Do you think I should meet him?" or "Do you think she REALLY likes me?" "Draft" would call me on the phone and talk for hours about how much he adored her and couldn't wait to meet her. After a couple months of chatting online and on the phone, the two of them decided to meet with some coercion from me on both sides. I encouraged their meeting because they both seemed so fond of each other. And for him especially—a truly sweet and romantic soul—I knew the meeting would be bliss... only, it wasn't.

When his chat room girlfriend drove almost eight hours from Tennessee to St. Louis to meet draft_of_shadows, all the doubts that people go through before meeting someone face to face came true for Draft. She decided she did not want to be with him and left within a couple of hours. He was DEVASTATED. He had met one other girl from online before, only to be used and left in the end. This time, he was completely heartbroken. There was an awkward silence about it online in Books and Literature 2, because many in our chat community knew what had happened, but Draft continued to call me because he needed someone to talk him off the proverbial ledge. I would get IMs saying things like "Thanks for letting me vent" or "You always make me feel better." I thought it was sweet and that he was a sweet kid, and I felt really bad for what he had gone through, as I had been left and used many times before, and I knew what that felt like. I began to think of him as a very good friend, and it felt good after all those years of not really having one. We could talk to each other about anything and everything—and we did.

Then one night, he told me what he *really* thought about me, and it scared me to death. Suddenly, this "sweet kid" who had become a good friend was now suitor. I almost stopped talking to him for the simple absurdity of it all. He was nineteen, recently moved back into his parents' house, and working as a sales clerk. I was thirty-four, a mother of one, renting a house from my grandparents next door. I knew right then and there that he could NEVER come there—I could never bring him into my life because everyone around us would be much too critical for a billion reasons. Besides, he lived in St. Louis, and I had lived practically on the same street in Ohio for most of my life. It was impossible. I didn't know whether to laugh or cry at his revelation, and while I was flattered by his crush on me and deep down had developed somewhat of one on him, I almost nipped things in the bud.

But, I didn't stop talking to him. Against my better judgment, I began to consider him my "boyfriend" for all intents and purposes, though no one on my end in my real life even knew about him. We exchanged letters, cards, and Christmas presents. We talked for eight or nine hours on the phone every night, and I would sneak calls to him during all of my breaks at work. I even caught myself scribbling an "I heart Joey" on my agenda at work (Joey is his real name). He talked often of coming to meet me, but I was terrified to take that step. I was convinced that one look at me in person would send him screaming... and I also knew I could not bring him to my home because my neighbors happened to be my family, and I didn't want them to scare him off or vice versa. Besides, there was always the deep down fear that he COULD be an axe murderer. With Yahoo chats, you never know.

However, just a couple days after his twentieth birthday, there was a perfect opportunity for him to come meet me. I was going to be safely away from my hometown at a film preview (my first published book had been made into an indie film), so I invited him to come along. It was the most beautiful weekend of my life. We barely left the hotel room. He was amazingly sweet, the first man I'd been near in nine years—he was, in fact, the first person I ever really kissed. Within hours of us meeting, he asked me if I'd ever consider marrying him. I laughed it off, but two days later, when he had to go back to St. Louis, it was like someone ripped off one of my limbs. I cried for hours and hours after he left. We had literally gotten so close from talking in the chat room all of those hours and through all the IM and emails that I had already fallen for him long before I ever laid eyes (or hands or lips) on him. He went back to St. Louis, grabbed a duffel bag of clothes, introduced me to his mother over the phone, and then had his family drive him clear back to Ohio the following weekend, where they met me briefly and ate lunch with us before he and I eloped (with my daughter in tow) to a nearby town to get married at the JP on March 10, 2005.

Everyone says it was too quick and that there is no way we could have known each other well enough to get married. After all, we talked online and on the phone for only two months, met and spent three days together, and moved in together and filed for our marriage license only a week later… but what they don't understand is that the relationship we forged online was much deeper than if we had met in some random encounter. There was no physical aspect to get in the way. By the time we first saw each other face to face, we were already deeply in love. We already KNEW each other on a very real level before we ever touched. And because you tend to find people online who have similarities, our differences melted away in a pot of insignificance. The age gap didn't matter because online you are who you are, regardless of age, gender, race, or anything else. Our relationship is challenging because we are from two different decades and two different states, but I think we are both still amazed that we accidentally found love in a Books and Literature chat room, and we'll be laughing about it again on our four-year anniversary next March.

Autumn in Ohio

TRUE LOVE

I was forty-seven when I met Larry on match.com. I had never been married. I'd been dating online on and off for many years on several sites and had been meeting some nice men and having mostly positive experiences. I had a few relationships, but I just hadn't met "The One." By the time I met Larry, I wanted to get married, but I was determined to do so only if it was with the man of my dreams. Otherwise, I was quite willing to stick to my single life—which was pretty great.

I wasn't too interested in Larry when he connected online with a "wink." His picture and his interests just didn't do it for me, but since he lived in my neighborhood and shared my political beliefs, I agreed to meet him anyway. He had just moved to LA and said he wanted someone to show him around. He suggested we meet for coffee and lunch if we didn't "gross each other out."

Right before I went to meet him, I reviewed his profile. (You simply have to do this so you remember who you're meeting!) I noticed for the first time that it said he was separated. That was a deal breaker for me! It was a rule I always followed to ensure I met "available" men; I didn't date any man who hadn't been divorced at least a year. I don't know why I missed that when I agreed to meet him in the first place, but it was too late to back out. The first thing I said when we sat down was "I just saw that you were separated! This won't work because I don't date married men." He told me he hadn't divorced after five years of separation because it was a hassle and he didn't want to get married again. I told him that for sure it wouldn't work out because I was ready to get married and that our date was a waste of time. He said he understood.

Then, we talked about other things. We had coffee and, having not grossed each other out, we proceeded to lunch. I agreed to join him for dinner the next night. I can't really say why because I didn't really analyze it. I think since I knew it wouldn't go anywhere; the feeling of no-pressure was really nice. I had a good time with him. I figured I'd show him a little of the neighborhood that night and call it "done." Then, I'd go look for an available guy.

We had an amazing dinner. The connection was intense, and I felt so good being with him. We laughed a lot and listened intently to each other. We realized we had a ton of the most important things in common. We shared a wonderful kiss— easy and very romantic. No man had ever looked at me the way he did, and it made me feel so good. He was a wonderful man.

The next day, Larry brought me flowers. Couple days after that, he told me he thought he was falling in love with me. I just took it in and didn't respond. We never talked about the "unavailable" issue, and surprisingly I wasn't worrying about it. It was so natural and just flowed. There was nothing forced or phony. I was just enjoying myself and—for once—staying in the moment.

The next week, he had plans to go back to Kansas City to complete his move to LA and see his granddaughter in her school play. (Another example of why I fell in love with him!) We talked on the phone every day, and when he returned, he came straight to my house from the airport. He told me that he filed for divorce while he was there. We had never even discussed that as a possibility. I was surprised… but then again, not really. It seemed so right. Even though we had only been spending time together for about two weeks, it just made sense.

We went on our first weekend trip the next weekend, and that was it. We were in love. We started living together a week later, got engaged in six weeks, and got married in six months. And remember… I was forty-seven and never before married. I was truly waiting for the right time and the right man. We have a marriage that most people only dream of. We both feel so lucky. Not only have I found the man I'll spend the rest of my glorious life with, I've completely changed my career and now help other women do what I have done—to find the kind of love that completely enriches and fulfills our already great lives.

<u>Lauren in Los Angeles, California</u>

CHAPTER 7

NIGERIAN AND RUSSIAN SCAMMERS, HOOKERS, AND MARRIED PEOPLE THAT PLAY

There will always be some people who want to take your wallet on a date and not you! Unfortunately, there are those who are sympathetic, possibly lonely, who are played for their emotions, seduced, and dumped by a scammer. If you have met a genuine person in your search for online romance, the subject of money should NOT come up for a very long time.

While it is possible the love of your life may not live near you, the reality is that most people who are serious about a relationship live within a reasonable distance. If someone wants to date you, they MUST spend time with you to get to know you. If someone lives hundreds of miles away, be cautious because it could be a scam. If they quickly profess how much they adore and love you but have never met you face to face, BEWARE. How can they love you without really knowing you? These cunning and mysterious criminals sometimes take a month or two to try and develop a relationship, flatter you, or maybe send a cheap gift or two. They are very skilled at building trust and know how to make victims fall in love with them.

The only motive is your money. DO NOT SEND MONEY! Whatever the sob story of sick children, health problems, or being stranded in a foreign place without money, it is most likely a lie. The handsome person in the picture you think you have feelings for is quite possibly just a stolen identity. The same person you have been emailing could very well be part of a large circle of organized Internet crime from Russia or Nigeria.

Nigerian scammers often pretend to be foreign specialists working abroad. They often upload attractive Caucasian photos and say they live in the US but are abroad on business. A majority of the online cons are female or pretend to be female. In either case, it's not long before they hit you up for money. They will be abroad, notably in Africa or other European countries. They will tell you their employer has paid them with money orders and they cannot cash them, and then they will send them to you asking you to deposit them into your bank account and wire them money via Western Union. Needless to say, the money orders are no good, and you're left holding the bag. You will be reimbursing your bank and paying the fees for the faulty transactions.

How many men have had sexy blonde Russian girls send those pictures of themselves in scantily, clad, and provocative poses? They are supposedly in another state, but the truth is they are in Russia. Ninety percent of Russian scams originate in the Republic of Mariel. There is an extensive criminal organization led by men who have others do the legwork, placing hundreds of profiles every day and conducting correspondence. Most likely, they work on commission like a telemarketer. Girls are paid a minimal fee to sit and pose for pictures and pick up money at Western Union. Scams cannot only hurt your finances, but your heart as well. There are two signs to run when they mention money and Western Union in the same breath. Be suspicious of broken English in emails when the picture is of a girl in a plaid shirt from the Midwest who should be able to speak better than that. Pay attention to inconsistencies in the communication.

Prostitute scams reveal themselves quickly. They do not waste time in letting you know what they are after. They usually solicit business online, using sleazy usernames and steamy self-descriptions. They will let you know what hotel to arrive at for the exchange program. Prostitutes show strong implications in their emails that they want to offer you something "yummy," but there is a price to pay.

"Married on the side" happens to be one-third of men dating online. They will post a dark or unclear picture because they don't want to be recognized. Your date might eventually ask for your number but not give you his. It's a red flag when he calls at irregular times or very set times around his regular schedule or convenience when he is able to get away. If you always have to leave a voicemail only to wait long periods to hear back, be suspicious. The tell-all sign is when he does not disclose his last name or home phone and never introduces you to his friends or family. Run, girl! He is married! There's also another type of married people that want to play—what we know as "swingers." These are couples that are not monogamous and share other partners sexually. Swapping partners has become more popular and deemed a sexual revolution, but only behind closed doors. I wouldn't be surprised if your neighbors down the street did not have some sort of swinging lifestyle! There is even group sex and swinger clubs, but is all under wraps and beneath the law. The most prevalent time for swinging was during the Flower Power era of the fifties and sixties, but it still exists today, and the Internet is a prime place for these kinds of people to find hookups with similar "hobbies."

SWEETHEART FROM OHIO

Richie's picture showed a jolly bearded man curled up on a couch with a cat rubbing his face. "Loving, caring, and hardworking" the profile said. When I received a message last January asking if I wanted to chat, I was so flattered. He seemed cute. We exchanged emails. He was friendly at first but quickly swelled in intensity and passion. By Valentine's Day, I had received a box of chocolates, a teddy bear, and a helium balloon that said, "I love you." At forty-six years old, I was hooked, even though we had not met.

Richie said he was from Milford, Massachusetts and that he was out of the country on a big construction job, helping build a stadium in Nigeria. As soon as he returned, he promised he'd come visit me in Ohio. He couldn't wait, and neither could I. Our spirited email romance hummed along for another two months before there was a problem. Richie said his boss paid him in postal money orders and that he was having trouble cashing them. He wondered if I could do a small favor for him and cash the money orders for him and wire the money to him in Nigeria. I agreed, and over the next two weeks, I cashed two $900 money orders and sent the funds via Western Union. Then, Richie was ready to leave the country, but he needed money to deal with visa problems. I cashed another money order.

My bank called, and something was wrong. I had to call a special number at the bank. Even then, I still believed this man. I had no qualms about the money orders whatsoever. Even after the bank told me the money orders had been altered and that they were purchased for $20 but then "washed" and doctored to read $900, I still held out hope. The bank told me I was responsible for the money. I had to pay them $2,700, which was everything I had. I was devastated and felt like my whole world was falling apart. All I could see was that adorable man curled up with a cat. Never in my wildest dreams would I have known that this was part of an elaborate online scam. He spent four months gaining my trust, and he did it. My world and heart were destroyed!

Anonymous

> *Unfortunately, this is not the first story I have heard like this and probably won't be the last. When we are truly in love or think it's a possibility, we as humans know no boundaries. Often times this can leave us dejected, damaged, and broke. I think it may be a good idea to take a page from the old modeling agency motto... if they are truly interested in you, you won't have to pay a dime.*

THE RUSSIAN TRANSACTION

It's interesting what you can find on the Internet. I met someone who had a beautiful picture, but it was definitely a generic photograph, and I wasn't able to see both sides of her face. She wrote me many times but with broken English. After the first several exchanged emails, she began to imply that she would like to be "friends with benefits" and asked me if I was interested in what she wanted. As a newbie on the site, I had no idea what she was implying, but she gave me her email, and I decided to meet her late one evening night.

The first thing she did was kiss me on the cheek. She was a beautiful blonde with a voluptuous body. I asked where she was from, and she said, "I am Russian and came here to this country to make a living for myself through a program. That is why I am on the dating sites in the first place." A light bulb went off in my head!

"Oh! So you meet with people who are your clients, and you get paid for sexual favors?"

""That is correct," she responded.

"So, that is why you wanted to email me pictures instead of posting them on the dating site?" I asked.

"Yes. That is correct," she again responded. I couldn't believe I had stumbled upon a Russian hooker and that I had been so gullible, not realizing what I had gotten myself into. First of all, I was not going to pay this woman for sexual favors, and secondly, prostitution is illegal in this country. I really felt sorry for this young girl who couldn't have been more than twenty years old. I bid her a good night and told her I was sorry, but I just wasn't interested in what she had to offer. It really was a shock, and I wanted to know more about it.

While researching Russian hookers on the net, I came across an abundance of websites that offer Russian women for marriage in exchange for payment. I also stumbled upon Russian girl dating services and many other sites. You read about Russian women, and the websites explain that all they want is a better life and they are not selective about their husbands. I found this extremely sad and unusual. People can actually buy a mail order Russian hooker bride? I couldn't believe it!

Mark in Atlanta, GA

THE SWINGERS

I was surfing online and met a young woman who sent me an email telling me that she was interested in having sex with multiple partners, and this sparked my curiosity. I decided to meet this young woman, and she explained to me that she and her husband were swingers. I couldn't believe it! I had never heard of a swinger before. She asked me if I would like to swap or engage with partners. She said it's a great way to experience something new and it allowed them to revitalize their troubled relationship. She told me that her husband's name could not be revealed because he worked for a top company. I found this very strange and did not want to go through with married people that wanted other partners.

She persisted, saying, "We want to find a trustworthy person." She explained that they both had wanted this for a long time and that group sex is amazing. "It first started when we went to strip clubs. We were drunk and ended up hooking up with a stripper," she said. She kept saying they weren't a threat to anyone, but they wanted total discretion because they had kids. They didn't want cell numbers involved. The couple had a shared private email address and could only text through email via carrier of the phone. I asked her if she thought she would be cheating on her husband while being with other partners, and she assured me it was just "part of the deal." She considered it occupational fun for all of us. She then told me that they were not interested in anyone underage, so I would have to verify the age.

I kept asking many questions because I couldn't figure out how swingers actually end up doing what they do? It just didn't make sense to me. She said the first step is to meet someone or a couple for coffee, the second is to exchange a make-out session with them, and the third is to meet again, but this time at a hotel. She said, "Don't get me wrong… my husband is the best thing that ever happened to me, but we just have curious and sexual needs that can't be met in a monogamous relationship. We are just very flexible and open-minded people. We all end up not just being friends, but sexual partners as well." Well, as hard as I tried to understand that philosophy, I couldn't quite wrap my head around it. I have heard many stories about men cheating on their wives or women cheating on their husbands or men letting women cheat on their husbands. I am even well informed with the whole Hugh Hefner lifestyle, but witnessing a swinger lifestyle was a first for me.

Anne from Long Island, New York

THE CHARMING CUBAN WITH AN ASIAN ACCENT

I made a profile on millionairematch.com, and before I even added pictures, a Spanish guy who goes by the name of Chris sent me an email. I couldn't believe it! I mean, I know I have great pictures, but since when does a handsome man randomly send you a message when you haven't even completed your profile? He told me he was the CEO of a construction company, that his last name was Valdez, he said he was widowed, and that he lived in Miami. I decided to Google him in which I found his website that portrayed his construction company and even a picture of his deceased wife. Everything looked factual and real. Since my mom retired and currently lives in Pompano Beach, I knew Florida well. I sent him a message back saying that I had just gotten back from visiting family in Florida but currently live a state over. After a few flattering filled emails, he got off the online dating site, and I never heard from him again until seven months later.

He emailed me back, but the email was really strange and written in broken English. He replied, "I am here now thinking about what next to do, and I am thinking of the possibilities of making it work with you... and who knows? Maybe you have find someone else, but if you not, i will want you to know that here i still think of you and i will want us to start talking about how to make it work, a little about my self to refresh your memory i own a construction company.. i have a daughter who is now 13 years. i will send her recent picture along in my email. I hope you are doing. please reply me as soon as possible for me to know what has been going on with you, so that we know where to start from now and i believe in family because families are always there thanks for your understanding." He sent me more messages saying that he had moved to the UK for business due to a bad economy and wanted to find a woman because his wife was deceased. He also talked profusely about praying to God, which I found interesting. However, I just thought he may be bad at emailing, so I continued messaging him, hoping to hear back from this handsome Spanish man.

He ended up sending me another email saying, "To the glory of God i got this construction contract and it was like a God sent gift. i will not tell you everything is sweet... sometime we laff, sometimes we cry, i need your help cos i am already out of cash." Uh huh I bet he is out of cash!

I replied, asking him how much he needed.

He responded rather quickly saying, "I need just $ 2,100 to pay my hotel bill, and if you want any id of mine i will send it instantly if that will give you more confident in me and if you do this for you name will never be out of my history book and i will always call you my angel. i will wait and see." I thought this was really sketchy. He actually emailed me his passport which was American. It looked like a real passport! He then gave me the hotel name, which was LAGOON in Manchester, United Kingdom.

I gave him my number, and he called me, and he definitely did not sound Spanish—more like Asian sounding than anything else I had ever heard! I had heard about these people before, the kind of people who lurk around the Internet like spyware. They send you fake checks, ask you to wire it to them, and then your bank asks you to refund the money because it's a fake check! But this guy was a bit ridiculous; asking me to wire him money via Western Union is a means for a disaster. I told him I lost my job and had no money, which was a lie, but I wanted to keep this ridiculous scammer on the line to see what other excuses he would come up with. Then his price decreased to $700.00. "Please, I must pay for my hotel bill," he exclaimed. His last response was, "Please, I need your help on Maria aspect ... I need your help in completion of her ticket please i don't know if you ever believe me but just look at it like you doing charity or helping someone please i don't know what else to do please. She need just $245 please send it in her name please send it true Western Union money transfer and please get back to me with the information please i am begging." The fact that this scammer spoke in broken English, was begging me for money, and was also asking me to wire him money instead of sending him a check sent up huge red flags. I told him NO and wouldn't you know, I never heard from him again. Adios, Amigo!

Lisa in Atlanta, Georgia

THE SEXY MARRIED WOMAN

During the late years of the nineties, it seemed that online dating was only used as a forum for meeting for sexual encounters. I had just gotten divorced and literally found a smorgasbord of beautiful ladies to select from on a website known as MySpace. I had met many women on MySpace before and had some great risqué and wild adventures with them, but I had never hooked up with a married woman before.

One day, a message popped into my inbox from a beautiful lady who seemed to be very prominent, sexy, and well dressed in her pictures. In the message, she said, "You are a strikingly handsome young man with a very sexy attitude that is portrayed in your profile. You sound like the kind of guy who likes to take a chance in a daring environment." I had no clue what she meant, but I was definitely up for a daring adventure. She was a little older than I was. She was thirty-eight, and I was only twenty-four. However, I decided that age didn't matter, and I had listened to the song "Stacy's Mom has Got it Goin' on," so I simply couldn't resist.

We chatted back and forth for a little while. She told me she had kids, and I explained to her that I was just fresh out of college working for a nice little company. She further explained to me that she was a lawyer and lived in a beautiful five-bedroom brick house with Brazilian oak floors, a Jacuzzi outside, and a new Mercedes paid for in cash. I thought, *Could this be my new suga' mama?"* I really wanted to meet this hot chick! We started chatting about sexual encounters and divulged our sexual fantasies to each other. It seemed that all she wanted from me was sex, and I couldn't complain.

We decided to meet at a quaint little restaurant right off the corner of a famous author's house. The restaurant was dimly lit with candlelight. It was near Christmas season, so the place was decorated with wreaths and Christmas trees. I suddenly saw her. She had already sat down, but to my shocking disappointment, there was an older man sitting next to her. She beckoned me to come and sit down with the two of them. I sat down, not sure who this other man was, but then she asserted, "This is my husband. We have been together for ten years, but we are comfortable being with other people. We believe that we will always love one another, but to make our marriage work, we both need to be sexually pleased, even if it is with other people, as long as we are honest with one another."

"I couldn't believe my ears! I said, "Well, that's interesting. I am really open and have had a lot of wild encounters, but none like this one. What is your proposal?"

"Well, we would both like to get to know you better over dinner, and then I was wondering if you'd like to have sex while my husband watches."

I couldn't believe my ears once again. I didn't want to be a wuss and bail out of this little idea they had going on, and I thought it was kind of kinky in a way, so I decided to agree to the rendezvous. "Well, I have given it a little consideration and thought. I would love to get involved."

During dinner, we all had pasta and lasagna while cracking jokes by a fire just behind us. They were asking me what they should get their kids for Christmas. Having just come out of college and not being a father figure yet, I really couldn't give them any brilliant ideas. I told them about my past girlfriends and how I really didn't know if I wanted to get married anytime soon. After dinner, they asked me to meet them at their house and told me their kids were out spending the night with their friends so we would have the place all to ourselves. I agreed and followed them to their beautiful house in the 'burbs'. As I entered the house, I saw a grand staircase leading up stairs, beautiful portraits of their family, old artwork from the 1700s, and a lot of old antiques. As I sat down on a red velvet couch, the husband turned on the news and asked me what I thought of socialism compared to the Republican Party. I told him I was a Democrat. He laughed and offered me a glass of wine. The wife came back down the stairs, laid on the couch next to us, and slowly took off her Jimmy Choos.

She turned on the stereo that apparently played in every room of the house and asked me if I wanted to come upstairs. After consuming so much wine, I eagerly agreed and followed her up the grand stairwell. The husband didn't follow us but instead was distracted by the news on TV.

Upstairs, she started to unzip her little black dress and began to unbutton my shirt and unzip my pants. Before I knew it, we were all over each other on her king sized bed covered with silk and linen sheets. She told me the sheets were Egyptian cotton and that they had bought them in Europe somewhere. Her husband soon came upstairs and watched us, walked away, and then came back to watch us again. I wasn't sure what his interest in watching us was, but I enjoyed having sex with her. I thought that maybe it was better for him than watching porn because it was real, right there in front of him. The married woman had a huge advantage. She was older, had much more experience, and was more passionate than any of the other women I had met.

We didn't stop until about five in the morning. She grabbed my hand and took me down a long corridor that had huge closets and bathrooms. She led me to the steam shower, and we laid in the steam for about fifteen minutes talking about morality and sex. We both got dressed, and she made breakfast for everyone, including her husband. They seemed like a lovely couple, and he hadn't portrayed a bit of jealousy over the night before. They laughed, talked about a new movie coming out that they should take the kids to go see, and asked me what I was planning to do for the rest of the week. I decided to meet this lovely couple again many times, and we all had fun just like our first rendezvous. I never stopped to think this was just a strange encounter, but I guess everyone has their own opinion on monogamy and sex. All, I can say is, thank God for MySpace and the older hot and married women that love to play!

Michael in Manhattan, New York

CHAPTER 8

MANNERS, LUCK, AND GOOD PROTOCOL

Regardless of what Hollywood movies portray, finding a long-term relationship takes patience, skill, and effort. Unfortunately, one of the drawbacks in cyberspace is information overload. People are unwilling to put up with the slightest imperfection and suffer from "the click problem" while browsing through a sea of faces on "the date menu." If a person is the wrong height, wears the wrong shoes, makes a wrong joke, or admits in an email that they are guilty of snoring on occasion, they are simply dismissed. A good sense of protocol and manners might defer one from being "clicked off" into the galaxy of cyber abyss.

Women want to be appreciated for something more than their looks and sex. They want a man to earn their affection (from soccer moms to CEO's-the vast majority of women still like to feel taken care of, especially on a first date). With that said, men often complain of feeling like an ATM machine or of feeling unappreciated for their efforts. They usually do not like it when, on a first date, a woman orders the most expensive item or wine without any consideration.

Men almost always operate in a "fix it" mode and are often unsure about what a woman really wants. Men can't read our minds. They often appreciate our verbal cues to help them figure out what we really want. This helps them toggle between a "just listen to me gripe" mode and a "honey, please help me fix my problem" mode when listening to us.

A little patience and tolerance just might bring a reward. Besides, do you REALLY want to be constantly back at the drawing board sifting through endless profiles. How exhausting! It's just too much work, so don't be too picky! You might find Miss or Mr. wonderful who might just be having momentarily bad hair day! If nothing else, good manners and behavior will lend itself into a potential "second date," and an opportunity to get to know someone better.

COFFEE BEAN AND A PENNILESS SURFER

As a young woman living in the city of Los Angeles, I enjoyed the perils of the cyber world and loved the online dating scene. I often speed dated several men a day! One particular day, I decided to meet someone for coffee. Ironically, a man had pinged me and asked me to join him for a cup, which seemed like a coincidence. He looked like he could afford me and was also a very good-looking guy with a sandy surfer look that drew me to him. I simply couldn't resist a harmless free cup of coffee with the pleasure of good conversation. I had decided to meet three people that day and he was first on the list. I drove my car down the street toward The Coffee Bean and waited for him to show up. He was ten minutes late. Just as I was looking around for his car, a public bus drove up, and to my shock, he stepped out of it. Apparently he had either lied about his income, or a horrible car accident must have taken place.

He walked into the Coffee Bean, plopped down next to me, winked at me, and told me I was gorgeous. I responded, "What happened to your car?"

"Oh, I don't have a car," he said. What in the world was going on? This was an absolute no-no in my book. *How can you not have car?* I thought. He further explained, "Well, I don't believe in cars actually." I was beside myself. *How does he get around Los Angeles? What does he believe in?* This was one strange man, and the situation could not get any weirder.

"Well, why don't we go ahead and get in line?" I asked.

"Yeah, that sounds like an awesome idea. I got a free coupon for myself since I am low on cash at the moment," he said. He wasn't even going to pay for my coffee!

As if that weren't bad enough, when we got in line, he ordered before me—a vanilla latte with extra cream, which he paid for with his crumpled coupon. The man at the counter tried to use it but noticed it was expired to which my date went absolutely ballistic. As we stood there in the long line with many impatient people behind us, my date went from arguing to shouting with the clerk. "If I don't get my coffee with that coupon, I am just going to steal it right out of the store!" he threatened. I was appalled and embarrassed. People were glaring at us like they were about to boot us right out of there. I immediately interjected and offered to buy both my coffee and his.

When we finally sat down, I asked, "How do you pay for online dating sites?"

"Well, my mom pays it," he retorted. *Oh my God... is he JOKING?* I wondered.

After painfully listening to his boring banter, I drove home, and needless to say, honesty about being a complete loser would have been the best policy. I mean, the guy's mother paid for his Match.com subscription... and it's too bad she didn't give him coffee money to save me the embarrassment!

Kim in Los Angeles, California

Wow. I mean, wow. The sad news is this unfortunate man will likely hang ten for most of his life, and find another woman, which his mother can pass the baton to. A great example, of how we as wives, mothers, and girlfriends can infantilize men at times. As women, we have a need to feel security. In fact, research shows that the need to feel protected and secure both financially and physically ranks above physical attraction in female needs. This guy not only sounds broke and lazy, but completely unable to control his emotions and feelings. Be thankful you emerged unscathed and stay clear of the surf!

LADY AND A COP

I met this lovely, yet dangerous woman online, and we decided to meet at Ruth's Steakhouse. Being a southern gentleman, I really wanted to wine and dine this woman.

We had an enticing chat over dinner, and she seemed anxious but very sincere and interesting. She was very beautiful, had a great rack, and was dressed to kill right down to her sexy shoes. She had a couple of glasses of wine with steak and lobster while

I had only one glass of wine. As we were departing, she said, "Oh gosh... I feel a bit intoxicated and am just not ready to go drive my car just yet."

I replied, "Well, I'll tell you what... I can bring my car around, and we can go grab a cup of coffee somewhere until you feel better if you'd like."

"Okay," she agreed.

I pulled out of the restaurant carefully, trying to figure out where in the world to go, and we got to the end of the road beside a park filled with trash and graffiti on the walls. She then exclaimed, "Why don't we just pull up by the park, listen to the radio, and talk for a while?"

This was a bit of a sketchy part of town, and I knew this park very well. It was inundated with hoodlums and other such activity. There was a gun murder case not far from the area that had happened about a few months prior. The park was always swarming with cops left and right, and I was sure they would be keeping an eye on anyone who set foot in the area. So I said, "Well, this particular park is not the best place to go. The police are always on duty in this area, and anyway, this park is always filled with seedy looking people."

At this point, my date got extremely upset and started testing me. She said, "Oh, don't get paranoid! Don't be such a prude."

"Um, I am being real serious here," I said. "The police are out to get people, even if they are just two people on a date and parked somewhere just to have a good time."

"Oh, don't be such baby," she retorted. I felt like she was really testing my manhood, so I decided to park, and immediately she started flirting with me. She then made some kind of comment about getting in the back seat of my car. I hesitated because I just knew if we played around in the backseat, we would surely be put in jail or harassed by the police.

I started thinking, *did she really wanna have coffee, or did she just really want to take me parking?* While I was thinking to myself, she said, "A *real* man would take me in the backseat!"

"You don't understand. I know the police here. You do not park in a sketchy park in the middle of the night without looking suspicious. They usually have donuts down the road and park here to make sure there ain't any riffraff going on."

Sure enough, as we were arguing, the police pulled in, turned their lights on, and told me to roll down the window. He took my ID, told me to get out of the car, and made me take a Breathalyzer test. He searched my car and everything inside the car, including my date. Then, another police car pulled up, and they all joined in the search. After all the unnecessary but expected harassment, the cop finally told us to leave, and I was happy to oblige. I looked at her thinking, *I downright told you so!* I took her back to her car, said goodnight, and drove my a—* home knowing, making no promises to ever call her again.

Mark in Atlanta, Georgia

Protocol Tips to Keep You on the A List:

1)   All in the eyes! Eye contact is sexy. It's an important window to the soul and quite flirty. Don't wear sunglasses at night or in a low-light atmosphere. Even in bright sky, at some point, take them off so your date can see who you are. Men, be careful. Talk to her eyes and not to her chest. Cleavage or not, you must be disciplined!

2) Wandering hands? Not a good idea on a first date. Any display of sexual or over affectionate touching is a no-no unless invited.

3) Talk the talk, or they may walk. Leave a bit of mystery because when you meet a stranger, they most likely don't want to know your whole life story. Don't discuss your exes or past relationships unless asked. Getting to know each other is fun and takes time.

4) Honey, I shrunk the kids—and brought them on our date. Bad idea! It diminishes your freedom to converse freely. Cancel your date plans until you can get a sitter, or at least give your date a heads up and let them decide whether or not it's best to reschedule.

5) Don't cyber rage if you don't get a response. It is a busy world, and people are overwhelmed and may not have the time to respond. Don't take it personally. If they are interested, they will show you by responding in time.

6) In the land of texting, one must refrain doing so during a date unless it's an emergency. There is nothing more of a turn off then when a date pays more attention to a phone that you. Do pick up the phone and call sometimes. There is nothing more exciting than the warm tone and expression of a real voice.

7) Cyber stalking. "Who has viewed me?" and your name and picture comes up fifty times in a few days. At that point, a person knows you are either crazy or crazy about them.

8) Humor and sarcasm is tricky and often misunderstood. It can lead to a negative impression, especially in text messages, IMs, online chatting, and emails. Save it for a real time that is face to face with that person.

9) Avoid profanity (even jokingly). At any age, people find it insulting. Another thing to avoid is using all capital letters in emails, for this will be taken as anger or shouting.

10) Intimacy is often the gage of whether to take down your profile if you have been corresponding and casually dating. Save your feelings and talk about them exclusively. If you have not been intimate, then it permits you to end like you began—via email.

11) Don't misrepresent. Everything on your profile should be honest and unveil the real you—your real looks, your real income, and your real likes and dislikes, and so on. It's disappointing to have expectations that in no way whatsoever match the information you have received from your date.

12) Too much alcohol can be a bad thing! Some men say it's their favorite scent on a woman's breath, but too much might delete you in their mind for a second date. Men, women don't like a drunken date. Spend your time impressing her with being responsible and contentious.

13) Weekend plans. Take it slow and get to know each other. If it's long distance and you travel to see one another, make sure for the first time to make your own arrangements at a hotel in case the chemistry is not what you fantasized it would be.

14) Keep your cell phone quiet and do not use it unless you have a true emergency and must take a call. Be attentive and focus on your date.

15) Communicate if you are really interested in a second date. Men, do what you say and say what you mean. If you are not going to call and have no intention, be polite without misleading.

THE BRIEF HOUSE GUEST

While surfing the net, I found this beautiful girl in Dallas, Texas. Since I had moved to the US from England, I couldn't wait to meet some new women in the area. She had twenty-three gorgeous pictures posted online, and they were totally intoxicating. I sent her an email, and we ended up talking on the phone for two exhilarating months. She just had such a warm personality and also had a high paying job that she couldn't get away from. Finally, she told me that she was getting some time off of her job, and she suggested that she come visit me. From her pictures, I could tell that she was wealthy because of the clothes she wore and the car she drove. I responded with, "I would love for you to come visit me, but it's quite expensive to fly over for one day, especially if it's just to meet me."

"Why don't I fly over for two days and one night? I'll get a hotel," she suggested. British or not, I am a very open-minded, and I felt I had gotten to know her enough through our communication. I really felt comfortable with this woman, and I have a five-bedroom house. I told her she could stay in one of the guest rooms. Her response was, "That is very nice of you. I'll do just that. I will go ahead and reserve the ticket and fly out for the weekend."

I couldn't wait. I was very excited and decided to get the house ready. I was going to make dinner by candlelight, have some flowers around the house, trim the garden, and get everything perfect. I drove through back-to-back traffic, which was a bit hectic, but arrived just in time to pick her up. I could see her coming out of the gate, looking for me wide eyed, and I started to walk toward her. I could see a resemblance to all the pictures I had looked at, but as she neared, I could tell that she was some years older than her picture, heavier but still attractive. As my eyes focused on her drawing near me, I could feel that there was something strange about her, but I couldn't put my finger on it. Her face was slightly off from the online photo. She just looked similar but different from the picture. The visual image of her just was not quite right in my mind. Something was different, but couldn't put my finger on exactly what it was. However, I picked up her bags, and we drove back to my house. While conversing, I explained to her that I had a weird and uncomfortable feeling about her, but I just could not figure out why. There was just something different about her pictures and seeing her in person. Even though she resembled the pictures quite a bit, there was something quite off.

She gave me a bombshell of an explanation. "Well, the pictures are really of my twin sister, who is thinner and looks prettier than me," she admitted. I couldn't believe what I had heard.

"Why would you do such a thing? Why wouldn't you put your own photographs on the website?" I interjected.

"I just felt like my sister and I are twins and we look alike, but she is just slightly more beautiful, and I get much more interested prospects this way. Anyway, my sister doesn't have as high paying of a job as I do." I was very startled and shocked that she would misrepresent herself and wondered what else she could be lying about.

I delivered her bag to the guestroom and said quite frankly, "We can enjoy each other's company tonight, but I'll be taking you to the airport in the morning to catch a plane home." It was a very uncomfortable evening, followed by an early morning with her not saying a word. I don't know if she felt rejected, but I had to be honest with her, and I just don't believe in misrepresenting yourself. Starting off with a lie on a first date always leads to further lies down the road. After I dropped her off at the airport, we never met again.

Bob in Atlanta, Georgia

"From groupies to roadies, Los Angeles to London I've heard all the BS fiction, but these erotic dotcom dating snippets are the real deal—like fake boobs you gotta live it to know the difference... and I have!"

—UKBOB WRFG 89.3FM

Five enquiries men should not ask on a first date: (Outrageous... but happens!)

1)   Are you a real blonde, and can I check?

2)   Are those breasts real?

3)   What drugs or medications do you take?

4)   What's your real age and number of divorces?

5)   Will you sleep with me and if so what are your sexual fetishes?

THE EXOTIC OCTOPUS

This certain individual I had gone on a date with was someone I had met online. My date, who we'll call Farzhad, definitely thought of himself as one wild and crazy guy. I showed up at Nic's in Beverly Hills and was 100 percent positive I knew who he was. He had to be the TDH (tall dark and handsome) guy sitting at the end of the bar, slightly smiling at me as I walked in. I mean, he sounded pretty normal on the phone, and this guy was wearing jeans with a blue pique cotton button up under a navy blazer, and sneakers. But, boy was I wrong. The guy I was supposed to meet was actually the one standing in the middle of the bar talking on his cell phone—the one in white jeans, a white linen button up (which he apparently only saw fit to use 30 percent of the buttons), a gold chain which appeared to be fighting for its life amongst the bushel of black wiry hairs covering it, and hair that fell in spirals like a mane around his face, obviously tied in a low ponytail at the beginning of the day judging by the crease that caused it to jut out at the nape of his neck.

He walked up and put his hand on my shoulder. He couldn't have been more territorial if he had walked up, lifted his leg, and peed on me (though that would have been especially gross considering his white jeans). We sat down, and he has already taken the liberty of ordering a martini for me. "What is a 'Li-chee?" I asked.

He got a smirk on his face and sort of laughed to himself and then said, "Lee-chee, my dear. Lee-chee."

I stood corrected. "Okay, then what is a 'Lee-chee'?"

He responded, "Well I don't really know, but they're damn good! HAHAHAHA." He actually cracked up at his own joke. The typical formalities of what-did-you-do-today ensued, and before I knew it, that creepy hand slithered its way back onto my shoulder. I did the casual oh-I-can't-find-something-in-my-purse brush off and began scrambling for a topic of conversation. He did not seem interested in talking. I asked him if he'd ever been married—"No." I asked him if he'd ever had a successful relationship. "Yes." I asked him why it ended. "It's too soon for us to be talking about this." *Okay,* I thought, *so it's too soon for us to be talking about past relationships, but perfectly normal for his hand to be generously slithering all over my spinal column?* I told him it wasn't my intention to make him uncomfortable (I mean, after all, why would I want him to feel like I was feeling with his disgusting groping ten minutes after meeting me?)

"It's just that talking about why a relationship didn't work often paints a good picture of a person. For instance, if you said 'Well, I was really into bondage, and her not so much,' then it would relay some essential information to me." I said.

He used a half-assed laugh as a sort of springboard to touch my waist and said, "Aren't you so funny," in an infantile-like manner, as if he were talking to a two-year-old who had just told him they "made a poopey."

He began to search for a waitress because his Lee-Chee martini has almost run dry, and he spotted one that kept walking by. He began to grow increasingly agitated until he was fixed in a full on-stare in her direction. Probably feeling the burn holes in her back, she made her way over to our table. Instead of just ordering, he decided to tell her where she went wrong. "You know, I looked at you several times to come over here, and you just kept walking by," He followed this by very passive-aggressive laughter.

"I am so sorry, she said. I actually just lost my contacts and can't see." You would think he would have been too busy inserting his foot into his mouth to continue with his rude hassling, but instead, much to my chagrin, he pressed on.

"Okay, hon', well we need two more Lee-chee martinis,"

I cut in, "Oh, no, I'm fine. I'm still finishing the one I have."

Again, he began the passive-aggressive laughter. "You might as well go ahead and bring her one. She'll be finished by the time you come back."

The girl, picking up on the absurdity, turned to me and said, "Would you like to hear about the other drinks or look at a menu?"

I ask her what else there was, and about three seconds into her response, this guy said to the waitress, "You totally don't want to be here tonight, do you?". There was an awkward silence.

Her arm promptly crossed over her chest in a subconsciously protective way, and her face flushed. She answered, "Why? Do I look that way? I am so sorry; I don't mean to look like that. I have just been really busy."

Being the a—* that he was, he felt the need to engage in that passive-aggressive laugh again. He then instructed me to take a few more sips and suggested we go to the Avalon pool bar. Why I agreed to this will remain one of the great wonders of the world, right along with the hanging gardens of Babylon and the great pyramid of Giza. As we were walking out, he simply puts his hand out, not looking back, and I was expected to grab it to let everyone in the restaurant look at his new acquisition. We walked out to the valet, and his Porsche has been pulled forward. We got to the Avalon pool bar, and he told me that I should order the espresso drink, and I told him that I don't like dessert drinks. "Well, then what are you going to get?" he asked.

I said, "I don't know. It's a tie between the sex kitten or the lavender lemon drop."

He responded, "Aren't you a sexy kitten? Give me a little meow, baby." I looked at him, waiting for him to move on to the next subject, but he did not. In the most annoying baby voice known to man, he instead rubbed my back and said, "C'mon… give me a little meow right here in my ear."

"Um, no," I said.

"And why not?" he had the audacity to ask.

"You give ME a meow," I retorted.

"Oh, you're feisty," he responded in a way that would make Austin Powers shudder. He began to tickle me right in the middle of this posh pool bar and said, "I bet you're ticklish." Unfortunately, I am extremely ticklish and unable to stifle laughter, which only served as encouragement for this creepy person. "We could just get hammered by the pool, baby, and have some amazing dinners. You should come. You'll come, it'll be fun." I felt like I was going to vomit.

You know how I know God exists? Right then, a waiter came up to us and informed us that the pool would be closing shortly and we needed to pay our tab. Hallelujah! Praise Jesus! We made our way out, and he said, "Hon', you've drank too much. Why don't you come back to my place and hang out for a bit?"

"No, thanks," I said. "I've only had two drinks in three hours, and I've drank a ton of water."

"Awww, come on. Are you scared I'll bite?" The creepy baby voice was back.

Again, I said, "No. Thanks for the invite, but I just don't go over to guys' houses on the first date." I quickly jumped into my car, which never felt so good, so safe, so welcoming, and so warm. I thanked him for a good time. He came up to the window and leaned in to kiss me goodbye. I go in for the peck, and just as I thought I was home free, he shoved his slimy tongue in my mouth. It began wildly going in circles like it was searching for something. My mouth was no longer participating in this kiss, and in some way, I could feel its resentment toward me for putting it in this position. I never felt so disgusted.

Colleen in Los Angeles, California

Five inquiries that women should avoid on a first date. (Believe it or not, it happens!)

1) Are you here to get laid or to find a relationship that leads to marriage?

2) What was your last girlfriend like and why did you break up?

3) How much money do you make and can I see your tax returns?

4) The economy really sucks; will you pay my bills or buy my Jimmy Choos?

5) When do you take a girl on a trip, shopping, or consider buying serious jewelry?

THE STUDENT THAT TAUGHT THE TEACHER

The town I lived in is a small one where everyone knows each other. I live in a little house next to a college that Eudora Welty, an author, made famous. I am an art teacher at a local inner-city high school not far from my home. Being a single mom with a small child in a small southern town, there is not that much to do but listen to some good blues bands, eat catfish, attend church, and visit with family. I love teaching underprivileged kids and seeing them grow. However, there was a personal void after a six-month breakup from a man I thought I was going to marry. How a good looking, passionate, and Latin-of-

Cuban-descent-from-Miami ends up practicing law in Jackson, Mississippi, I will never understand.

Feeling a bit unfulfilled, I decided to surf the net for a date. I met a few men for lunch, some gentlemen for dinner, and a few for drinks. I had been talking to this guy who didn't have a picture posted. It was intriguing because he stated in his profile that he was a professor in pre-law at Millsaps, a prestigious college. I thought, *Perfect! He's geographically and professionally desirable—it'll be just two teachers with a lot to talk about.* We decided to meet at Finnians, an Irish pub midway between my house and Millsaps College. He knew what I looked like, but I never got his picture. "I'll find you at the bar," he said in the last email.

I was sitting at the bar excited to meet the college professor, and there was a tap on my shoulder. I turned around to find a kid! I mean, he was IN pre-law, not a teaching it! "Whoa! You're hardly a professor," I said.

"Yeah, I am really a student but couldn't help but be attracted to your picture. You're gorgeous," he responded.

"I'm 35 years old," surmising his age must be about twenty or so plus a year or two.

"Well, age is nothing but a number, and anyway, maturity is not defined by age, ma'am." He was absolutely gorgeous with thick curly hair and sparkling blue eyes.

Heck, I deserve to have some fun, I thought. We drank beer, ate fish and chips, and talked. I had to admit that my ego was definitely stroked. I actually found that my dad had done some auditing work for his uncle's law firm on State Street. One thing for sure is that in Mississippi the circles are so small you could suffocate just from a lack of oxygen.

It was getting late, and he wanted to follow me home to make sure I got home safely. I knew better, but he was so good looking with such a chiseled body. I wouldn't mind kissing this kid goodnight. OK, all these cougar thoughts kept running through my mind, especially since my little cub was with his dad for the weekend. This kid was raised right because he bought dinner, followed me home to make sure I was safe, and kept calling me ma'am, which I had told him not to even though I did appreciate the respect. He even asked me if I would like him to come in and check the house out and turn on the lights for me. *Hmm, how could I resist his gentlemanly manners?* I thought. "Sure, darling, come on in for a bit," I said. We sat on the one sofa, and one thing led to another, and one thing led to another led to another, and we were making out.

"I'm a virgin. I have never told anyone about being abstinent but I'm so attracted to you, I could just lose it right here with you, right now," the college kid exclaimed.

I could not believe what I was doing! Was this right? Was this wrong? Hell, I don't know because I hadn't been with anyone since Victor, the man I almost married six months ago. In a New York minute, this kid (a virgin) was mastering the art of seduction without any "how to" education. He didn't seem very shy. He seemed to know exactly what he was doing and how to do it very well. This was either exceptionally raw talent and skill or he was just lying. Whatever the case, at that moment I didn't care. The next morning I looked over at the kid and glanced at the mirrored reflection of a woman's face that had been truly satisfied. I looked up and said a brief prayer. "God forgive me, for I have sinned." I then went to the kitchen to put on a pot of coffee.

Leigh in Jackson, Mississippi

CROCODILE DUNDEE IN NEW JERSEY

The fiasco of Internet dating continues in earnest. I had stopped for a while, feeling mildly discouraged. I can't recall whether it was me who contacted "The Australian" or whether it was he who reached out to me. Regardless of who started it, we began a dialogue online, which quickly became a telephone contact. Rather than waste more precious time, we scheduled a meeting. I assumed it would be coffee date; he assumed it would be dinner. We met at an ethnic restaurant, and he gave me a hug at hello. I wasn't repulsed and thought this might be a good sign. We sat down, and he did the ordering for the two of us without asking what I liked. He brought out two bottles of wine and immediately cracked open the first one. *So far, so good,* I thought. He had a lot to say, mostly about himself as he poured his glass first.

I am not much of a drinker, so midway through the wine, I began to feel more relaxed. I always enjoy hearing about other cultures, and he was more than happy to share with me fun facts about his country of origin. The dinner progressed with very few, if any, of the typical first date "uncomfortable silences." I was now feeling a glimmer of "wow" creeping in. He was pleasant and friendly. He shared with me some details of his recent first date with another woman he'd met online. She was a police officer, and from what I recall, he felt she elaborated too much on her job. He related that he could not wait to get away from her after the meal. Shortly thereafter, I attempted to make a joke, stating that I wanted to tell him more about my work history. He didn't get the joke, and there was our first heavy silence. Following our shared meal together, he seemed game to continue. We were both a tiny bit buzzed from the wine (or at least I was), and it was a pleasant evening. Since we lived relatively close to the beach and the weather was nice, we agreed to drive to the beach and take a walk.

Once we hit the beach, he reached out to hold my hand. I was not feeling like we were at the hand holding stage, but I held it anyway. We stopped to take our shoes and socks off, and the ocean was warm on our feet. The moon was out, and the setting was perfect except for one thing: I wasn't feeling it. I wasn't repulsed, but at the same time, I also wasn't feeling like I wanted to touch him. The wine buzz began to wane, and now I had sand sticking to my feet and my legs and I knew I wanted to leave. Instead, we walked the boardwalk and watched all the people. I wanted coffee, and he wanted more wine. The differences between us were now blooming rapidly. We finally made our way to the car, and he presented me with the second bottle of wine he'd brought along, informing me that we would drink it "on our second date." I acquiesced and agreed to a second date the following weekend. Why did I make a second date when I somehow already knew it wasn't happening between us? I think I was unable to face the necessity of bowing out in person. Cowardly comes to mind. He leaned over to give me a goodnight kiss. It was not a sweet kiss, for it had a bit of the tongue lurking there. This was not good. I was not ready for the tongue. I was uneasy with this plan, but considering he was the only man I had gotten past a first date with, I thought I needed to try harder. I ignored the nagging little voice in my head telling me this was a no-go. I thought maybe I was too quick to rule him out, and I would try again.

The Australian telephoned me the following day to confirm our dinner date for the weekend. We met at the restaurant for our second dinner together. He ordered the wine for us both, and this time I chose my own dinner. The hand reappeared to take mine. This rapid intimacy would have been welcomed if I felt it was reciprocal, but I did not want to be holding his hand. I thought perhaps I needed more wine. The conversation sunk to a new low when he described his hunting days and the joy he felt when shooting kangaroos in his country. I am not fond of the whole hunting thing. I understand its nature and, in fact, he explained that kangaroos are often dangerous the way deer are here in New Jersey when they run into cars on the highway (or vice versa). Nevertheless, the thought of this man blowing away a kangaroo made me feel less than amorous toward him. He suggested I accompany him to a play, along with his cousins, in two days. I stammered and felt myself like a deer caught in the headlights. Again, too cowardly to say no, I agreed to the date to go to the play, this time with him and his family members. I was now miserable. I did not want to go to the play with the kangaroo killer, but somehow I had just verbally agreed to do so.

Following the dinner where I tried to avoid eye contact with him, I broke the cardinal rule of having the second date. I did not know where to go with him after the dinner was over, so we returned to my house, which was close to the restaurant. I know, I know—I should NOT have brought him to my house; particularly if I knew I was not interested in him. Besides, he could have had the Crocodile Dundee big knife wedged somewhere. Despite all this, we came to my house. He immediately cracked open that second bottle of wine from our first date and proceeded to criticize the fact that I did not own wine glasses. What an insult! I did have champagne glasses, but that was not adequate. He informed me that he planned to buy me new wine glasses in the near future. Frankly, I didn't want wine glasses. I was perfectly content with the amount of glassware I currently owned. However, for a man who believed he was a wine connoisseur, this was clearly a social faux pas. Despite this error in presentation, he proceeded to utilize the incorrect champagne flute and promptly finished off the bottle of wine. We played several congenial games of backgammon. He was now ready for the big make-out scene; I was not ready for this at all, and after a few awkward kisses and groping, I extricated myself from his grasp and explained he was going way too fast for me. I told him that in my past life, I would have been right there with him; however, as a now presumably "mature" fifty-five -year-old, I preferred to have intimate relations with someone I actually knew. (What a concept!) He was somewhat perturbed with me but begrudgingly allowed me the option of discontinuing this session. I am certain he believed he was laying the groundwork for a future romp if he did not push the issue. I, in fact, was certain that there would NOT be another session with this man. This thought became cemented in my mind when he then announced that he was probably too intoxicated to drive home. *Okay, how manipulating,* I thought. Now this annoyed me. On our second date, he was now suggesting that I allow him to spend the night. This was not what I was interested in. I informed him that I did not wish for that to occur. Suddenly, he was able to drive, and off he went. My sigh of relief was short lived, for he reminded me that he and I had to soon meet again for the play. The play was scheduled for a Sunday.

The Friday before, the Australian telephoned me and stated he was in the area and wondered if he could drop by. I was at home doing absolutely nothing. My head told me this was a bad idea, but I was bored, and there is a part of me that finds it fun to have a male pay attention to me—even a male I am not interested in. This is a terrible admission, I know but I went ahead and told him to stop over. In he walked with a fresh bottle of wine and the announcement that he and I would take a trip to the local mall so he could purchase me those wine glasses. I began to think he was some kind of glassware control freak. I took a deep breath and recited those useful four words, "I don't think so." I proceeded to tell him that I did not think this was working out between us. Mr. generous "I want to buy you stemware" turned into Mr. Hostile. He got very angry and somewhat mean with me. His offense lost its oomph, however, when he shared with me that he had, in fact, been dropped off at my home that evening. (He had no vehicle) I asked him WHY, and he stated that his cousin felt he had been drinking too much to drive. "And is that true?" I asked him, incredulously.

"Oh, yes," he confirmed. "I am drunk."

So, okay, here are the facts: 1) this man clearly had a drinking problem 2) this man came to my home without a vehicle in an intoxicated state (how did he think he was getting home?) 3) This man was hostile to me when I suggested I did not wish to pursue this relationship and 4) this man was a known killer of cute kangaroos. Enough said. I told him to gather his bottle and I would drive him to his home, which I did. In the twenty-minute ride, he proceeded to alternate between telling me how great I am to what a terrible person I am. This reminds me of the moral to my story: try not to date men with drinking problems, and try not to make subsequent dates with men you are fairly certain are not for you. Just before the Australian left my vehicle, he told me that I did not have to still attend the play with him if I did not want to. I did not want to. I was clear in that message. He slammed the door, and I watched him stagger away. This was the closest "successful" Internet connection I had made so far. Oh dear! Not a good sign at all.

Meryl in Toms River, New Jersey

Ahhh the disease to please. If Meryl could only have been comfortable with feeling uncomfortable for a few moments and telling this drunken Aussie "no" the first time, she would have gained hours of her life back. Sometimes it is important that we identify our feelings and articulate them to the other person, even if they are hurtful. Peace at all costs, shouldn't mean hurting ourselves. G'day mate!

CHAPTER 9

NAVIGATING THROUGH A JUNGLE

"Our greatest glory is not falling but getting up every time we do"

—Confucius

Help… where are you Tarzan? These animals are pretty wild out here! Yes, our entire dating landscape has changed, thanks to the Internet. Our mind-boggling options are endless, and our attention span and level of commitment are fleeting. Marching through it all while thinking you can escape without getting pounded, bitten, or stomped on is an anomaly! Social networking, websites, and hot tech gadgets keep us constantly engaged, yielding lots of little moments of connections; be it a flirt, a wink, or a bit of happy babble in the form of an email, a tweet, a status update, or phone conversation.

They can last through a glass of wine, an entire meal, or even a budding relationship… but then they can vanish without any explanation. The cold hard truth is, you WILL get disappointed or have war stories. However, the end result of finding "The

One" is worth the effort. You are a prize! Be observant with a keen flattering strategy. In other words, don't put up with any crap. If you're not seeing the results of a loving relationship with respect, feeling cherished, experiencing deep passion, joy, trust, and loyalty, then listen to your intuition of the missing signs. Delete the toxic waste!

WILD WOMAN ON FIRE

I started online dating looking for the right woman after being married to and divorced from the wrong person. I had found a woman online before, married her, and it ended in a terrible divorce. However, I had high spirits, and as anyone who's southern and positive would say, "Heck... get out of there and find that right kinda gal for you!" I really am not the kind of person to search for someone to clear some kind of emptiness or a gap in romance, but I am a business man and just don't have time to go out and date. I would never go out to a bar and pick up a chick, and I wouldn't randomly hit on someone while I was out playing tennis or golf either. I am either with my clients, at work, or with my two children. Online dating seemed like the organized and decent way to have an overview of people before you decide to go out and date them. That seemed adequate to me.

Sifting through many beautiful women (and there were a lot to pick from), I saw one that I decided to message. I was a bit apprehensive since I had endured a jungle of either crazy, deceptive, or sleazy women. Only a few that I had come across seemed well put together and normal. This girl's profile seemed normal, but she seemed like a hottie! She was gorgeous, blonde, and it seemed like every picture in her profile portrayed her doing some kind of sport—white water rafting, paintball, or skydiving. This gal looked super adventurous and hot too! I pinged her, and she messaged me back a couple of days later saying, "You are a very cute guy, look adventurous, and seem like a southern boy, looking at your profile."

I replied, "Well, I am a southern gentlemen and would love to take you out to dinner!" She looked so wholesome, sweet, and seemed like the right kind of girl for me.

We arranged to meet at a dimly lit Chinese restaurant where they serve the food in front of you. I waited for her for about ten minutes and thought, Boy, am I hungry. I could totally go for some shrimp, chicken, and rice right about now. She showed up, and my hunger instantly went away. She was tall, thin, stunning, and really young looking. My jaw almost dropped! I really didn't want to screw this one up, so I stood up, greeted her, and pulled out her chair. We started wining, dining, chatting, and I noticed that she didn't seem to be too intellectual. I also noticed that she kept asking for sake shots and was drinking her wine rather quickly. I just assumed she was nervous, so I tried to concentrate on the categories she was interested in talking about.

I quickly learned that she was definitely not that bright. She kept dropping her fork every now and then and eventually, after two many shots, she looked incredibly drunk. She even fell off her stool! I quickly glanced around and noticed that almost everyone was watching. Then, out of nowhere, she said, "I can put my nipples on fire!"

"Uh, really? How did you learn that?" I asked.

"Well, my stripper friend showed me how." I thought to myself, I can't believe she's serious. She further explained, "Well, it involves like a chemical preparation. You rub it on your nipples, and it just sets them on fire!" I sat there cracking up laughing and thinking, "Hmm... definitely not bulls—!" She began to rub her foot around my ankle underneath the dinner table. As we are conversing, she interrupted the conversation and said, "I am planning on rafting down the Chattahoochee in nothing but a thong because that's how we do it back in California. Whoo hoo!" she screamed. OK, it was obvious this girl was very buzzed from too much sake. I couldn't believe this girl was serious. Wow, the picture certainly failed to reveal the wild child she seemed to be.

"Why don't we go back to your place, turn the lights out, and I'll come out with flaming nipples," she said.

"Does that come with whipped cream?" I asked, laughing.

"If you want it to, Mr. Sexy Man," she responded. I thought, God, this is really aggressive behavior for such a sweet and wholesome looking girl. I truly wasn't looking for a one-night stand, although I am sure many guys would have gladly taken her up on her offer. I kept thinking if I invite her to my house as drunk as she is, she might burn the house down with her flaming nipples! I began to wonder if there would be a second date with this wild child.

I ended the date with a peck on the cheek and wondered if I should ever meet this strange and wild girl again. I met my friend for lunch and asked him for his opinion. "Well, Scott, after everything I told you about the date, what do you think?"

"Well, I think you are a very mature person and don't think she's the right person for you. She seems a bit wild if you ask me, and that ain't wife material."

"Well, I don't know. Don't you think she'd be fun at parties? Wouldn't you want my girlfriend to set her nipples on fire? She could be the life of the party."

"Well, there's someone to send home to Mama," he retorted."

We never made it to a second date.

Mark in Atlanta, Georgia

SHINY BALL SYNDROME

The male I am going to tell you about is one of the most predominant of the Los Angeles Dating Species (LADS). You may have come across this type yourself. Upon first meeting, he presents himself as the total package. You begin to wonder, why would this species ever need the help of an online dating service such as Match.com? Then you realize that Match.com is simply supplementing his already robust dating rotation.

I got my first email from Johnny Rosenthal when I moved to LA at the beginning of March. It simply said, "How are you this lovely day?" Now, keep in mind, if a guy sends me some half-a—* question (or worse... one of those impotent little "winks"), I don't give their profile a second thought. Why would I if they can't do the same for mine?

That being said, ole Johnny had a very intriguing profile picture. He was obviously tall, and it was some skilled photographic shot of him at a poker table playing what looked to be a pretty high stakes game. Given that I dabbled in a little blackjack to put myself through undergrad, my interest was piqued.

I checked out what he had to say in his profile, which was not much. Ladies, this is a Match.com red flag. It usually means one of two things: 1) they are unable to create anything of substance to say about themselves or are horrible spellers, or 2) they have only signed up with this service to poach and prey with no real intention of letting anyone get to know them for a significant period of time. For these types, it might as well be Bootycall.com.

Being somewhat subconsciously privy to this theory, I guessed Johnny was the latter. He seemed like a pretty intelligent guy, so I knew it wasn't for lack of substance that his profile was leaving something to be desired. This predator had thrown down the ultimate online dating gauntlet, and I was ready to accept the challenge that lay ahead—to convert jaded California Jew Royalty Bad Boy to Reborn Committed Boyfriend.

I wrote and asked him why he was on Match.com, and his only response was "Uh, for the intrigue." Hook, line, and sinker. Johnny Rosenthal met me at La Poubelle and was fifteen minutes late. I caught this TDH (tall dark and handsome) throwing the keys to his 2009 Jaguar XF to the valet and talking on his cell phone in typical LA Jew fashion. Motor Trend called this car "flat out sexy," and I would have to agree. The driver wasn't bad either.

He hugged me and gave me a peck on the cheek (I'm learning that this is a common greeting along the west coast). He sat down and ordered a full on meal—steak, potatoes, bread, and a glass of scotch. I was sitting with a MAN. I didn't if it was the XF, the unconcerned use of the valet, the exorbitant menu at La Poubelle, the casual I'm-not-that-interested-so-I'll-carry-on-a-conversation-on-my-cell-while-greeting-you, or the fact that he was drinking scotch on the rocks, but I was at once completely at peace in my security blanket of father-daughter relationship recapitulation.

Johnny was able to carry on a conversation. We were both entrepreneurs (he was an accomplished one at that point) and had a good talk about that. We talked about politics, and he was definitely well informed. Johnny walked me to my car after a few hours and said he had a good time. As I drove home in blissful euphoria, I launched the idealization activation sequence, fully intending to fill in all the gaps of the things I didn't know about him with things I wanted him to be. As soon as you do this, you are cooked. Admit defeat. Throw up the white flag. Great athlete... incredible cook... brilliant kisser... phenomenal in bed... loving, caring dad... devoted husband. I was DONE—hooked like a crack addict—and we'd only discussed current events for the past two hours.

Johnny texted me twenty minutes later to say he had a really good time. He called me several times that week, and we planned to go out to dinner at a great little Italian restaurant called Pace (pronounced "pa-chay") in the valley. We arrived in style and would valet as usual. I imagined us doing this every night. Everyone there seemed to know him, and he seemed to sort of haphazardly wink when they would come by and say hi. Again, our conversation began taking on the nature of a White House interview vs. a date. The look-at-me-Daddy dynamic was in full swing.

Johnny had an obvious cold. He was completely stuffed up and opted to not drink wine because of his cold medicine. This told me that despite him being physically ill, he still wanted to see me. At the end of the night, he dropped me off at my door, gave the usual hug, and told me he didn't want to get me sick and skipped the California peck on the cheek. He called me a few more times that week. He was asked to throw a charity gala and was a bit apprehensive about doing it given his father's advice not to. I think I received one more call from him later that week. We talked about the event, and he said it went well. There was no talk of going out again though. He just sort of told me that he was going to be going out of town for a while, in New York for work for the next two weeks, and then he was planning an ice fishing trip to Alaska with his dad, and then he would be in Cabo for a friend's bachelor party. It sounds like he had obtained the concept of "shiny ball syndrome." In other words, he had become fixated on one toy for a brief bit, but when her "shininess" wore off, he was off to the next one. Translation? "I've found a new shiny ball, and I'm going to chase that now. Thanks for playing."

Colleen in Los Angeles, California

This is the classic, good looking, and successful player plagued by attention deficit when it concerns women. We all have fallen prey to these types. Chances are unless he develops real intentions desiring a meaningful relationship with depth; he will chase "the shinny ball" long into dentures and old age. Even age and maturity can sometimes elude these charmers who tend to have a history of short lived or uncommitted romances. Looking at his past is a good prediction of a future. Better the shininess tarnish quickly saving you from an emotional investment that ends up highly disappointing.

BAD NEWS CLUES
(A WOMAN WHO IS INVOLVED WITH A
MAN WHO ISN'T INVOLED WITH HER)

1) He can't schedule anything more than a day or so in advance. If you hear "Let's play it by ear" constantly or "I can't make plans in advance," chances are that he is juggling, and you are convenient.

2) He calls late at night or shows up at your door drunk with "Honey… Sugar… Baby" on his lips—endearing expressions you never hear when he is sober. He wants SEX and not a relationship.

3) He is never available or interested in meeting your friends or family. He never introduces you to his friends. He has no curiosity to open the photo album on your coffee table because he doesn't care about your past—and he probably doesn't see you in his future.

4) He leaves you wondering about everything. What plans, if any, are there for the future? Does he have any feelings for you beyond physical ones? Don't be clueless! As Paula Abdul said, "Girl, don't play the fool!" Men are not complicated and are task oriented. If he wants you, you will know it. The phone will ring, and emails will show up!

5) It takes him longer than twenty-four hours to return your call. Unless he works for the CIA undercover and you are a security risk, he is blowing you off. You can almost bet he's finding time to chat with "Platinum_Pam" and "NakedMaid4U," trying to get a date.

You do not have to put up with bad behavior or a jerk. It's not your job to turn a narcissist into Prince Charming. Assess the potential, and if there is none, then move on. There is always the sea of proverbial fish, and the best catch is yet to be found.

CRAZY WOMAN AND A WATER HOLE

I am a Doctor, originally from New York, and was giving lectures in Austin and didn't know anyone. I met this young woman online, and we started chatting, bada bing style. We talked for a few weeks, but I was disappointed since it showed on her profile that she lived in San Antonio. I was so enthralled and riveted that I had to fly this gal out to Austin. I wrote, "We have talked for a few weeks. I would love for you to visit me, and I could get you your own room."

"Well, if I am not interested in anything intimate, then I can take my own room," she replied.

We arranged to meet on a Friday since I was giving my lecture on a Thursday night. She changed her mind and decided to drive from San Antonio to Austin on Thursday night and meet me in the late evening after my lectures around ten. After work, I decided to meet her at the bar in the hotel I was staying at for the time being, and she looked absolutely beautiful. She was wearing a velvet red dress that fit snugly around her voluptuous physique. I thought, WOW! She is knockout gorgeous! I invited her into my temporary abode, and we drank one of the most euphoric brands of champagne.

We ended up on a leather couch, and I asked her if she would like to go out since we had just met. "Why don't we have a couple of glasses and introduce ourselves," she suggested. We started kissing, which turned into heavy kissing. I honestly felt that I knew this woman so well because we had talked numerous times on the phone. I felt some kind of immediate chemistry during our display of current action. We ended up chatting, kissing, and drinking to the point of being somewhat intoxicated. She then whispered in my ear, "I've got to tell you this. I don't have my panties." I was a total gentleman, but I assumed this may be a queue to make another move. Fifteen minutes later, we had made it to the bed, and I felt we were so compatible.

The next day, we woke up, and she decided to show me around different parts of Austin that I had no clue about. We drove around to the beautiful capital, had a delicious breakfast, and went for lunch, and then she decided that we should go to this famous natural spring swimming hole. I am from New York, and it sounded like a redneck swimming hole that all the locals know, but I thought, Hey, I'll go if she wants to go. I reminded her, its 113 friggin degrees in Austin today anyway! Let's go!" We decided to go back to the hotel, and she started to tempt me again, so we fooled around all over the hotel room, and with no hesitation, she lured me into the shower. We had the most empowering, uninhibited sex.

After our wonderful rendezvous, we got into our bathing suits, and she decided that she wanted to take her car. We went downstairs and hopped in. The strange thing was that the car was in HORRIBLE condition. I couldn't believe what I was hearing! The brakes were like metal against metal. I thought, you have got to do something about this car. This is absolutely dangerous. I kept hearing this ear piercing sound every time we stopped at a light.

"This is dangerous," I exclaimed. I got on my iPhone to look for a place to fix brakes in Austin and found a place a mile and a half from where we were. "Why don't we go to the swimming hole, and then afterwards, we can drop off the car and rent a car, and I will take us back to the hotel," I said.

She answered, "I can't afford it. I don't have any money. I'll have to find some family member or an ex boyfriend to take care of it." In the back of my mind, I was willing to pay for the problem because I felt bad for the poor girl, especially for her safety. However, I didn't say this to her. I honestly didn't say anything because I was ready to get out of the damn heat and into the water hole at the moment.

We finally got to the swimming hole, and I realized I had forgotten my wallet at the hotel. The guy at the counter by the swimming area was going to charge us $5 to get in. I looked at my date and said, "I am so sorry. I didn't realize it, but I have forgotten my wallet at the hotel. Do you have an extra $5?"

"Well, let me go back to the car because I left my purse in my car," she responded.

As I was waiting there, I was melting. The temperature was just getting hotter and hotter. I was looking at my watch and thinking, Wow, it's been fifteen minutes. Obviously she did not have five dollars. Then twenty minutes went by. I finally lost my patience and went to find her, but she and the car were gone. I couldn't believe it! I was in my bathing suit and tank top with no money, and to top it off, I didn't know where the hell I was. I tried to call her, and she didn't answer. I texted her, and she didn't answer. I decided to call the hotel, explain the story, and ask them to send me a car. "Well, she has already come to the hotel and gotten a key," the hotel concierge explained to me.

I retorted, "Well, you better send security up there!"

As I was waiting for my car, waiting to hear back from security, and sending text messages saying, "What the hell did you do? You left me stranded,"

I finally get a response back from her saying, "I think we are after different things. You didn't even offer to pay for my brakes!"

I texted back saying, "You know what? I am a doctor. I am very smart but don't read minds and am not telepathic." I was thinking, what was I supposed to say? Every time a woman says she can't afford something, am I am supposed to pay for it? I finally got to my hotel and was amazed that nothing was stolen, but I couldn't believe this woman I had met online had fooled me! I was a total gentleman the entire time, and I believe she was just one crazy woman to have left me on our first date stranded in my bathing suit, a tank top, no car, no idea where I was, and no money!

Bruce in Atlanta, Georgia

THE LONELY ACTRESS

I entered the cyber world of online dating due to my hectic schedule and lack of time to look for someone the old-fashioned way. I have heard that a lot of people find someone at weddings, bars, church, kids' soccer games, and many other places. I felt that dating online was much easier since you come across a plethora of profiles that catch your eye. I went on plenty of beguiling dates that turned out to be either a dead end, a short-lived relationship, or a decent friendship. Although I had not found The One after a year or two of online dating, I still felt that I had made many social connections and developed loving friendships.

One day, while checking my email messages and surfing the net, I received a message from a beautiful woman who asked me if I'd like to meet for coffee. I found that she seemed quite assertive in meeting me, and I also thought she looked a bit familiar, but I didn't find that unusual because when you are living in Los Angeles, there are a lot of famous people whom you instantly recognize. I decided to meet her at a coffee shop near where she lived and drove down to meet her. I entered the coffee shop at ease, sat down with her, and we began to chat about our lives, have a quick banter, and exchange online dating stories.

All of a sudden, she mentioned Connecticut, and it clicked! I felt startled and hesitated for a moment. "What's wrong?" she asked.

"Well, I was supposed to call you twenty-five years ago."

"What do you mean?" she responded.

"I have a sister-in-law who lives in New Haven, Connecticut. I was there when she was marrying my brother, and her father told me to call this wonderful young woman because she was his accountant's daughter and was a famous actress out where I lived. He gave me her number, and I took it home, but I felt weird just calling out of the blue. The thing is, it was you! I didn't want to call you because you were all over TV."

"Well, I am rather glad I contacted you and we decided to meet," she said with a modest tone and a sweet voice.

She asked me what my sister-and-law's name was. I gave her the name, and she said that it was her father's stockbroker who had the exact same name. This was the girl I was supposed to call twenty-five years ago, and somehow she had found me on Match.com without knowing it. She began to tell me how lonely it was for her during the many years of playing a star on a television show. She exclaimed, "At first, It feels like you are on an adrenaline high. It seems like a dream at first. After a while, it all gets repetitive. It begins to get hard finding real friends, and you end up watching television alone because you begin to stop trusting people. Fame is only surface deep because so many people are shallow and dishonest."

I couldn't believe that she had truly felt this way. I thought to myself, this is just such a small world.

We went on a dozen dates and truly got to know each other. I learned a lot about the life of an actress, the brutality of the media, and the depth of celebrity life. She had finally retired from her acting career and was able to really start dating. In the end, we became friends and are still friends until this very day. It was wonderful listening to her perspective, thoughts, and situations during her past years. I learned that her happiest time was retiring from acting and starting another whole new different lifestyle. I was glad to have met her, even if it was twenty-five years later.

Larry in Los Angeles, California

THE LATIN LOVER

I thought I would take a break from online dating and wanted to meet a man, someone actually knew. I was introduced to a charming Latin man via email from a friend and decided to meet him at a business mixer on the west side of Los Angeles. I was just starting a consulting business, and he offered to help me and introduce me to some of his business contacts. At the end of our meeting, he spontaneously asked me out on a date. His looks, mannerisms, and style reminded me of the former love of my life (who didn't turn out to be that at all). He cancelled our first date, which isn't usually a good sign, but rescheduled it several weeks later. On our first date, he told me he was looking for a meaningful long-term relationship. He had been married before and hoped to be married again—music to any woman's ears! We continued to date, and on the fourth date, he arrived with two dozen roses, dressed in a tuxedo ready to escort me to a James Bond themed gala. I felt like a Bond girl with my real-life Bond. We danced for hours, and the chemistry was noticed by everyone at the gala. It took four weeks before we embraced with our first kiss. He was such a gentleman, and it was worth the wait. Shortly thereafter, a real love affair started to grow.

When Valentine's Day arrived, he planned a romantic trip to a five-star hotel. He said,

"My darling, you don't need to bring anything but your tooth brush." He was right, for we hardly left the room, as he had an elegant gourmet dinner delivered, complete with champagne and chocolate covered strawberries. It was such a romantic start to our love affair. We had talked before about an overnight trip and had the commitment talk. We agreed to be exclusive. It seemed we both wanted the same things, and every moment together was special. He told me that he had never felt this way about a woman before, and I believed him. He kept making plans for the future by scheduling dates and vacations. He saw me in his life! He told me he wanted us to spend more time together and he missed me when we were apart.

While I was clearly falling for this man, I failed to notice some odd behavior. We never spent two nights together back to back in a weekend. We would also only see each other once or twice during the week and no more. I never spent the night at his place, which I thought was a bit strange. Suddenly, he started making up excuses about work and family commitments and would cancel dates at the last minute. He would disappear for days and then suddenly reappear. I was starting to wonder if he was a real-life Houdini. Putting two and two together, I realized I wasn't the only one. I wanted to give him the benefit of the doubt, but my gut feeling said to drop him. I saw the red flags. A woman's intuition is very strong, but I chose to overlook them. He invited me on a romantic trip to Acapulco, and I accepted. That was where he confessed to me, "I have fallen in love with you." It was romantic and sexy while we were skinny dipping in our own private courtyard pool amidst the floating hibiscus flowers at the Las Brisas Hotel. When we returned home, he confessed that if he had a ring in his pocket, he would have proposed on the spot. Now, wouldn't that sound like a commitment to you?

Shortly after arriving home, while I was still aglow from our romantic trip, a friend called me to say she saw my Latin lover's active profile on Match.com. I hadn't even unpacked my bags, and there he was fishing nonstop online, probably offering the same trips and lines to other women as the ones he had offered me. All the sincere feelings he professed just didn't matter. I could no longer trust him. He was BUSTED! I found out later he had been juggling several women the entire six months we were dating. I realized I had been played by a masterful player, and with tears in my eyes, I sent him an email saying I was moving on. I was done.

A few days later, one of my neighbors told me she had seen my Latin Lover embracing another woman in the lobby of a fancy hotel while I was out of town. Somehow, I wasn't shocked! The lesson I learned is that talking about monogamy and exclusivity when horizontal with your clothes about to be tossed off doesn't count. In other words, have the talk while sitting fully clothed in a chair before you pop open the bottle of champagne. It might have more meaning. He was always an in-the-moment guy, but apparently he was in the moment with several others as well. In retrospect, I have saved myself the heartbreak, made a smart decision, and kept moving forward.

Julie Spira in Los Angeles, California, (excerpt from *The Perils of Cyber-Dating: Confessions of a Hopeful Romantic Looking for Love Online*)

Oh the gold chain, oh the chest hair! If only this Latin lover did not fulfill the stereotype. This is unfortunately so very often the case with too-good-to-be-true dates. Oftentimes, especially when things are new, we tend to fill in the gaps of the things we don't know about the other person with the things we want them to be. The truth is usually that they probably are not as great as we first make them out to be.

This is a great example of how one should always trust their gut instinct. Julie knew something was amiss and as such, took her head out of the clouds long enough to see what was truly under the surface. Although painful, this is the only way we get to the truth, and more quickly find genuine and lasting love.

CHAPTER 10

IT'S A NUMBERS GAME!

"Better to have loved and lost then to have never loved at all."

—Ernest Hemingway

Risking you're heart in an attempt to find compatibility, attraction, friendship, and trust in a mate is often a journey of trial and errors—sometimes a lot of errors. Love is not finding the perfect person, but seeing an imperfect one perfectly. Sometimes timing is everything. You might have the right person but at the wrong time. Boiling the complications of finding "The One" down to numbers of attempts, successes, and failures may sound unromantic but it is a reality except for the lucky few who immediately hit the jackpot and find Mr. or Mrs. Right. Online dating offers a greater opportunity than you would ever have in the real world. The good news is that you are out of your normal social and work circles into a broader range of choices. With the economic slowdown, online membership has spiked 20 percent from 2008 to 2009 and continues to rise! With a few thousand new faces online and at your fingertips, your chances of meeting someone just went up!

The bad news is running numbers. Casually dating lots of people sometimes gets too task oriented and burdensome. Don't despair though! It only takes that one lucky number for happiness. Think of it like cold calling. For every 100 numbers you dial, you might actually speak to twenty-five people, and of those twenty-five people, five might be interested in what you have to offer. I know it sounds futile and overbearing, but it's worth it! If you are talking to forty people in one month, assuming that probably more than half of them are definitely not right for you, then you really only have about ten to twelve people that are potential matches for great chemistry. One out of twelve might end up in a relationship scenario. Thus, it is really a one in forty that is possible for a "love match." However, that's just in one month! You see, finding love does take work. Get on the proverbial rollercoaster with that mouse in hand and click away to increase your odds. You might just find your "love match!"

A TWISTED LUCK OF FATE

I used to be the queen of online dating. I had the typical crazy ones (the maulers, the proposers, the nuts, and many others), but really, the most touching was with the guy who ended up becoming my husband Dave. During the first three weeks that we were seeing each other, I played very hard to get. I kept canceling our dates and refrained from kissing him whenever he courted me on dates. I wasn't trying to be coy, but I was moving 500 miles away a few weeks later and didn't want to get into a relationship that wasn't going to go anywhere. So, I told him that we were just friending. I thought it would be best not to get confused and begin a relationship that would be stagnant, or to fall in love and then have my decision altered.

One night, I made him an extravagant dinner. We had a great conversation, and we decided to head out to a small local bar. As we were seated, we heard this young man get up and sing with his band. I'd never met this guy before or heard of him, but he'd written a song that *was* inspired by a book written by my dad, When God Winks: How Coincidence Guides Your Life, and I wanted to hear it. His sister had attended one of my dad's book signings, and she just happened to be talking about it to him. From that conversation, he wrote the song that he performed that night. When we got there, we learned that his wife was best friends with my husband's brother in high school. This seemed like a strange coincidence. I suddenly felt like mine and Dave's lives were more intertwined than I thought.

Something shifted for me that night. I suddenly felt more intrigued by this man and felt more connected with him. We began to become inseparable, and two weeks later, Dave told me that he loved me. I confessed that I loved him just as much as he loved me. Three weeks later, he took me ring shopping just in case the opportunity ever presented itself. I still made the decision to move 500 miles away, hoping that a long-distance relationship would work out. Moving so far away didn't change a thing! I felt like I became even closer with this man, and he came to see me every few weeks. Our romantic relationship bloomed and became stronger and stronger. A year later, he proposed on one knee and gave me a box with the same ring that I had picked out many months before.

Robin in Maine, Massachusetts

Independence From The British

This story begins with the website Plenty-of-Fish.com and a guy we'll call ""Hugh." For those of you who don't know, POF is another online dating website, but unlike most services, it is free. However, it can serve as a good ego boost because as a female, you can get up to fifty emails a day. One guy in particular's picture struck me. He fit my type to a tee—chin length, dark, wavy hair, olive skin, dark eyes, athletic build. To top it all off, he was from England and had one of those accents that makes everything they say sound extremely intelligent.

We agreed to meet on Tuesday for dinner. I'm pretty sure it was love at first call when I heard his voicemail message. His accent was incredibly sexy, masculine, confident, charming, and clever. He picked me up at my place and delivered as promised—fit, tan, gorgeous, and very British. He was holding a piece of paper with the directions to my apartment, and I noticed that he was still looking at them when I got in. He said "Uh, right, get in cahhh… check! Say hellooo… check! Ask gull where she'd like to go for dinna…" as if the slip of paper contained instructions for how to go on a date. Sense of humor… check.

From that moment on, he put me at ease. I don't remember ever being self-conscious about my outfit, hair, makeup, or anything. He was completely interested in everything I was saying, and the feeling was mutual. Hugh was educated as a solicitor (British term for lawyer) but was in a lawsuit with his previous firm and was opening an online store for field hockey gear. His mom called, and he apologized and said he had to take the call. I thought this was very endearing and didn't think much of it. Later into our meal, he said that his sister was actually in town from England and wanted to know if it was okay if she joined us for a drink. I agreed, and we all hit it off. His sister was just as charming as he was, and I immediately was in awe of my date. He was gorgeous, British, witty, and had an obvious loyalty to his family.

He walked me to my door and told his sister he would be back in a minute. I showed him around my apartment and the view of the San Diego bay, which was pretty spectacular at night. He turned me around with complete ease and kissed me as if we had kissed 100 times before. It was magical. He told me he would like to see me again, and the only thing I was able to muster was a head nod.

Throughout the night, I kept waking up to a dream. Did that just really happen? He kept texting me throughout the night with "I feel like tonight was a dream. It almost doesn't feel real." It was clear that we both were in lust. The next morning, he did not play any games. He IMed me through the computer and told me that he and his sister were having tea. We sent YouTube videos to each other of the things we thought were the funniest. He called an hour later, and we spent another hour on the phone talking about everything from relationships, to family, to the British version of The Office.

Despite him being with his sister, the two of them met my friends and me at Rock Bottom Brewery the following night for a drink. It was clear that this was something that wasn't going away soon. Like magnets, if we were within two feet of each other, we were immediately glued at the hip. Being with him felt like one of those good sleeps where each time you turn over, it just feels better and better.

I could do no wrong with Hugh. He liked me unconditionally, and I didn't lose my personality while I was with him, as I tended to do with other men. I was fully Colleen, and he accepted all that it was. We didn't play games. We called when we felt like it. We saw each other every day. He invited me to watch him play on that first Saturday (he was on the US Olympic field hockey team because he had dual citizenship). The catch was, his parents were visiting from England.

It seemed a bit strange to be meeting the parents within the first week of dating, but he didn't seem to think a thing of it. I agreed and they were cordial, but I could tell Mama Bear was not to keen on other females (especially an American) in her son's life. Hugh remained unfazed. We went out with his teammates for a celebration that night, and he showed no interest in talking to them. He told me that usually he would be looking at other girls in a bar but no one was attractive to him anymore. We were glued to each other all night as if there were no one else in the bar. He asked me to be his "gull friend" that night, and I said "yes." There was nothing else I would have rather been in that moment than his "gull friend."

That night, interestingly enough, both of our exes texted us. His was named Claire, and he said they had dated for two years but that she treated him horribly and only would call when she was bored. I didn't have a thread of jealousy. I knew where his heart was. At "dinna" the following day, his family asked me what I planned on doing after graduation, and I told them I was planning on taking some time off and traveling in Europe. I had saved up some money, and wanted to explore a little bit before jumping into a post-doc. I could feel Hugh's anxiety in the room, and the moment we were by ourselves, he asked if I wanted him to travel with me.

I thought this was a great idea and knew my parents would be much happier that I would have a travel companion, and Hugh volunteered his parents' home in England as our base. It was perfect. My life was perfect. I had gotten my education out of the way, and now Mr. Right had showed up at the perfect time and was going to help me tie my life into a perfect little bow. (Can you see where this is going?)

Hugh traveled home with me for my graduation the next month and saw where I grew up. He met my mom and then my dad. It was a little anxiety provoking, but he got through it. He loved Indiana and couldn't quit stating his shock over the low real estate prices (you can buy an estate there for around $400,000, whereas in California, that is the median cost of a very average home). He mentioned the idea of us settling down there in Indiana. He dropped the L-bomb and told me he'd never felt this way about any "gull" in his life. This guy was really serious, and nothing about that scared me. He was clearly into me, and for the first time, I wasn't running the other way. Everything seemed perfect.

My friends at work (all psychologists by the way) began to show their concern about my relationship with Hugh. "The whole thing seems to be moving rather fast, Colleen, and he doesn't even have a job." It wasn't a great concern for me to convince anyone other than myself. I was happy, and that was all that mattered to me.

Hugh was pretty much living with me at this point. He began bringing over his laundry and doing it at my place. He ate my food, drove my car, and used my gym, my Ipod, my bath products… you get the picture. He would drop me off and pick me up from work. During the day, he would typically go back to my place and sleep after dropping me off at work. He would wake up, eat, and then go to the gym. He would go back to sleep and sometimes would forget to pick me up at work. He would get mixed up with directions, and one day I ended up waiting two hours for him to find me. I thought it was cute that, like me, he was book smart but a bit ditzy.

He would make major mistakes with money and dates, and I was the one paying for them. He did not have good credit (I think if I had just run a credit check at the beginning of this relationship, it would have saved me time), so I had to front a lot of his expenses with my credit cards. I bought his plane tickets back and forth to England, Indiana, Paris, and Argentina for his hockey tournaments. He got the dates wrong, and we had to reschedule and pay $700 in fees. At this point, he owed me close to $3,000. One night, I was in the bathroom and noticed that there was a prescription for Zoloft in his man bag. I asked him about this, and he immediately denied it, saying, "Oh, I never take it." The silence became very loud, and then he said, "Okay, you want to know the truth? I was diagnosed with OCD, and I take it to calm down those thoughts, but since I've been with you, I haven't felt the need to take it."

At the end of June, he helped me move all my stuff out of my apartment and into a storage unit. We put some of it at his place, and we took off for England on July 1. We spent several weeks at his parents' home, and he told me that he would like to wait to travel until he could save up some money. Around mid-August, we went to Paris. He slept most of the time, and when he was awake, he did not have enough money or energy to do much else. Although we were in the most romantic city in the world, I had never felt less romantic. I started to wonder if this was all there was. We had sparks flying at Rock Bottom Brewery and couldn't even get the light on in Paris? Mother nature's six-week veil was beginning to lift, and the truth was starting to rear its ugly head.

After spending months in rainy, cold, dreary England, I was bored to tears. I even wrote an entire book on "happiness," ironically. The days went by, and he seemed to have no motivation to do any other traveling. I began to grow restless and eventually told him that I would be going back to the States in September—with or without him. This caused an uproar in the house. His mother, who had not completely cut the chord, was biting back and saw me as the American enemy, the "gull" that would take her son away from her.

He was torn between two women. I reasoned to myself that I loved him but would not stay with a guy that couldn't stand up to his mommy at thirty-four. I told him that we would do whatever we needed to do to make sure that he saw them. If that meant that we would fly back and forth between two countries, so be it. September arrived, and we both flew back to the States. We lived together at his place until he could "save up some money" so we could move out on our own. This was a first for me; I never lived with a guy before. Living together was great. We woke up together, had tea out on the porch, went to the gym together, had lunch at Panera, talked about why people are the way they were, went to the grocery together, grilled out together, and sat on the porch over many, many dinners and laughed over exaggerated scenarios. We were best friends, yet passionately in love with each other. He knew about each of my girlfriends, and when I returned from a night out with them, he was there with the kettle brewing, ready to hear all about it.

During that time, he still did not have money. He was still driving my car, using my envelopes, stamps, food, gas, and everything. He still had not paid one cent toward the $3,000 he owed me. He did not have A/C in his house. He did not have a house key to lock his door. He did not have a washer and dryer.

He didn't have a driver's license. His car was not drivable. He would get lost going to the gym. He would need to go to Bank of America each day and check his balance because he couldn't figure out how to get a username and password to check online like every other person in 2008. He would get lost on his way to the bank. The man did not even have an Ebay account. He was over 30,000 pounds in debt, and there was no clear idea as to how he was going to get out. He was a puddle. My family warned that this was not likely to change and that I may always have to support him. My father told me "This guy is playing you for a fool and will take you for everything you're worth." I reasoned that what he gave me in return emotionally was worth the investment. After all, I put myself through school for all those years, so I wouldn't have to compromise when it came to my love life, right?

Even so, I had a talk with him and told him about mine and my family's concerns. He became defensive and said, "You know I'm not just some sort of Lothario. I really do have a plan to get out of this." However, I noticed that he wasn't making any efforts to amend his situation. He would sleep for most of the day other than the daily gym run. He wasn't really doing much with his online business and would spend his days watching Kitchen Nightmares or Most Haunted on my cable television.

November came, and he was to travel to Argentina and then Germany for hockey games. He would be staying with his family in England in between trips. I thought this would be a perfect time for him to come to grips with what he truly wanted. I imagined him sitting in dreary England by himself and missing me. Without the comforts that America provides (like unlimited refills, Panera, Chili's, and ice in your drink), he would soon realize what he wanted, and that would provide him with the incentive to work hard to correct his money situation. I couldn't have been more wrong. We talked less and less as he was away. I told him it felt like he couldn't wait to get off the phone with me. He told me I was crazy and probably just felt weird because we had not been apart that long. I agreed and went on with life.

In December, he returned, with his sister in tow. The week he was back was odd. He wasn't overly enthused to see me and really seemed to avoid any alone time together. He would keep checking his phone and had difficulty maintaining eye contact with me. I knew something was up. I confronted him again, and he said that it was just me. He seemed to react with an incongruent amount of anger, as if to start a fight between us that would never end. Christmas was approaching, and I thought an iPhone would be a great gift for him. We would have free mobile-to-mobile, and finally, he would not have to use mine every time he went to the gym. We went to the store, and as the guy asked him to get his membership number from T-Mobile, I noticed as he was scrolling through his phone that there were several text messages from Claire. I pulled him aside and asked him what was up. He denied everything and said "Aww, babe, it's nothin'. We'll tawk 'bout it when we get to the cahh." We returned to the baffled man at the iPhone store (sister still in tow), and my gut was unrelenting. I could not proceed. I pulled him aside again and said I would like to see the texts. After all, we were going into a two-year contract together. He reluctantly agreed and gave me the phone but then hesitated.

I grabbed it and began running. I didn't care how insane it was. I knew that I would never have a chance to see the truth again. I saw texts that said "I really fancy a hug from you right now xxx" Hugh grabbed the phone from me, but it was too late.

I had already seen all I needed to see. Whatever else was on that phone, he was making sure I did not see it. I looked in his eyes and saw a complete stranger. Who was it that I'd been living with all this time? Had he completely duped me? Was my father right? Was he a Lothario? My logical brain made the decision. He cheated, and you two are done. Like a robot, I went to a hotel. My phone did not ring all night. I thought for sure he would be calling to profess his undying love, to say how sorry he was, and explain it was all a mistake. But there was nothing... only silence.

The bellboy must have took pity on me and brought me a glass of wine to settle my nerves around eleven that night. He seemed a bit scared when he gave it to me, as if putting a piece of meat in shark tank and yanking his hand out before it was bitten. I looked out my window at the city I was getting ready to leave. My hotel room felt like a coffin. The air was thick with deception. The world as I knew it was no longer a place where good prevails and good guys always win. I dreaded the morning when I would wake up to this reality again.

I returned home to my family to hibernate and heal. I am not sure how I would have survived without them. My life was not going to turn out like I thought. I was going to have to eventually get out there again and jump back in the shark tank known as the dating world. I was going to have to make myself vulnerable again and hope that my personality wouldn't vanish when I began to like them too much. I was single again. But this time, it was not a good type of single. I had lost my independence. All vitality of my girlhood, all my spirit, and all my laughter and unending optimism about life was stripped away by this person. If I could be deceived so easily, it could happen again. I couldn't even trust myself, how could I trust someone else? Months passed and I never heard a word from this person, who once said "I'm going to look after you." This person who had supposedly fallen head over heels for me and was discussing real estate in Indiana, now felt like an apparition. I felt like one of those women on Dateline talking about how she wired thousands of dollars to a man in Kenya who claimed he was a doctor and needed the money to complete his education. As time passed, my hopes that he would show up on my doorstep and explain everything began to fade. I reframed the situation and was thankful that I was only out $3,000 and not $30,000. I became grateful that I had not married him or had children with him. I was free and no longer able to be hurt by him any further.

I realized that in my quest for a "happy ending," I lost my independence. I lost that part of myself that serves as a barometer for reason. I lost the independence that even in a relationship, allows you to know the world will not come to an end if this does not work out. I sacrificed my values and beliefs in hopes that if I "bent" enough, he would choose me. My existence would be validated through a relationship, the ultimate confirmation that someone else has given you the seal of approval. Like one of those chameleons whose tail grows back when you chop it off, my independence and dignity have slowly started to redevelop. I'm not sure if that same unyielding optimism and innocence will ever return though. I may go scurrying in a cave whenever I meet someone that immediately likes me a little too much, but now there is a deeper sense of me. No matter who comes and goes, I will always be with me, and sometimes that has to be enough.

Colleen in Los Angeles, California

The phrase "fitting a square peg into a round hole" comes to mind here. This cad was a gold digger from the beginning but his British charm and good looks was probably enough to gloss over that a bit. That is, until she was buying bagels, diet cokes, stamps, etc...

It is the case for so many, that when we think we find true love we are willing to go to the ends of the world to keep it. The problem is that true love should not be that much work. True love does not cost money. True love does not cause feelings of doubt. True love does not know geographical boundaries.

Love is a verb, and as such we can't expect to just passively sit back and let it happen. Yet, if we find that we are the ones pulling most the weight—it is time to step back and take an objective glance of why and what we are doing.

THE SWEETHEART

From what I've heard, online dating success stories are few and far between. Friends and associates have shared their experiences—not horror stories, but about having trouble-finding people they connected with and about mediocre dates. I, on the other hand, loved the time I spent on Match.com. I tell people that my only regret was that I didn't stay active on the site longer!

I signed up for Match a few months after I ended a long-term relationship. I wanted to meet a lot of men, go on a lot of dates, and have a good time being single. Going online seemed like a good way to do that; I knew that I would have better chances of meeting and interacting with people, than if I were to see them at the bar. I chose Match because I thought it was the best way to meet my objective. The site has no religious affiliations and no endless questionnaires to help you find you're most compatible mate, and that appealed to me. I thought, Bring on the big random pool and let me sort through it.

It worked out swimmingly. I think the fact that I didn't have any expectations or desires to find my true love was part of why I enjoyed it so much. It also felt good that I had so many positive responses to my profile. I never ended up searching for men because I had plenty of inquiries to choose from! I went on a number of good dates with men whose company I truly enjoyed. There was one bad date; I wasn't particularly interested in the guy but let him convince me to meet him. The conversation was awkward, and I swore I would do a better job of trusting my instincts from then on.

There was one guy that I really liked, and oddly enough, he happened to be the first person to contact me. We emailed a bit and spent hours on the phone. He was smart, funny, sarcastic, and worldly, and from his photos, he was pretty easy on the eyes. We agreed to meet and hit it off right away. I was torn between wanting to spend more time with him and wanting to continue my footloose and fancy-free dating ways.

Eventually the former instinct won out. I told some of the other guys I had been talking with—even those I hadn't been out with—that I was logging off because I had become involved with someone. Everyone was kind and supportive. "You're a great girl... it's been nice talking with you... I wish you the best... he's a lucky guy." I was so pleased and surprised at how nice and responsive my would-be dates were. A few weeks into my relationship with Aaron, my mother died. Though we hadn't been together for long, he took the week off work and came to all the traditional events. He met many people that I normally wouldn't have introduced him to. He was there for me in every way.

A life-changing event like that really ups the ante in any relationship, so most of our friends and families weren't surprised when we got engaged only ten months later. We married a year after that and celebrated our one-year anniversary in August. I owe it all to Match.com.

Candice in West Bloomfield, Michigan

THE DISSAPEARING ACT

I met this woman on an online dating site who became someone I started getting very romantic with and endured a deep connection with. She was beautiful and sweet. We spent our weekends together away from our kids and had a lovely couple of getaways. We definitely had a wonderful time, and she seemed to have such a great sense of humor. We finally bit the bullet and decided to get our kids together to meet one another. Everything went fabulous!

I really started caring for her and decided to take the next step and planned a spring break vacation for us, including all our kids. We decided to go to the Florida Keys, and I paid for everything. I had learned that she had financial problems and couldn't afford the trip, but I didn't want to cancel. We did have a good time, although I noticed that she seemed to expect top room service, to stay in a nice hotel, and to go out to the grandest restaurants in the Keys. I paid top dollar for snorkeling with the kids, deep sea fishing, and swimming with the dolphins.

A couple of weeks after the trip, I had been invited to a huge opening party in Las Vegas. I wanted her to come with me, and she definitely obliged. I flew us out to Vegas, and all the celebrities were there. We saw Jessica Simpson, Arnold Schwarzenegger, Paris Hilton, all the Playboy playmates, and many other celebrities. We stayed at the hotel with many of my friends and their girlfriends. Everyone went out to the pool, and at one point, two women that worked for Us Magazine came out to the pool and were flirting with everyone. They ventured toward me. I was trying to be nice and respectable, but my girlfriend started yelling at them. To my amazement, she then turned to me and said she wanted to go to a pool that had some hot male babes called The Palm. Assuming that she must have been jealous, I agreed that she should go and have fun. I don't control anybody. I let whomever I date do what they want to do because I trust them.

That night, I excused the outburst, we made love, and everything was dandy. We decided to go downstairs and we were watching all the celebrities, the paparazzi, the limos, the Lamborghinis, and the food being passed around. I turned to her and said, "You look a bit hungry. You should eat something."

"I am not crazy about this food." I thought, this is gourmet food. I mean the food ranged from lobster, sushi, steak, and salad to amazing desserts. Everything looked edible and grand to me.

The party began to get a little wilder and more fun with the DJ and all the stars dancing beside the pool and snacking on all the desserts. Around ten o' clock, my date exclaimed, "I am hungry."

"Well, hun, there's food everywhere. There's fish over there, steak over in that corner, and deserts over there," I responded.

"I just don't like the food here. I want to leave and go eat somewhere else," she said.

I thought to myself, I just took this girl out for a $300 dinner yesterday, and the same food she ate is swarming around this party. "Hun, I have been waiting for this party forever. I am not leaving to take you out right now, but if you are that hungry. I will take you to the food court down stairs."

She said, "Sure. Why don't you take me to f—* McDonalds?"

She then walked off in a really angry mood. I decided that I'd have to just take her to the food court because I was not going to miss this party that I'd been waiting on for so long. I told my friends that I would meet them back there after I took her to get something to eat. We walked toward the elevator, got in, and as we are on the level where the food court was, I got off, and she stayed on the elevator with her arms crossed. The elevator went back up, and I couldn't believe what was going on. She was exhibiting such strange behavior. I get to the first floor, and she was nowhere to be found and wouldn't answer her cell phone. I tried my hotel room, other floors, and finally the party, and she wasn't there.

I decided to go to the casino, and then head back to the party, and finally my hotel room. It was around one a.m., and I was in the bathroom tidying up, getting ready for bed when I heard her open the door. "Where have you been?" I asked.

"I don't have to take s—* from you," she responded.

"Excuse me? What the hell are you talking about?"

She responded with, "You are an a—hole."

I had no idea what she was talking about, and I don't like fighting, so I just went to bed. She looked at me and said, "I have had it. I'm leaving." I couldn't help thinking, this is one strange woman. She either just wants someone who pays attention to her every second and spends every dime on her, or she is just plain crazy. I didn't care at this point and I heard her pack her bags and leave.

An hour later, she came back into the hotel room looking completely smashed and screaming at me, "You're an a—hole. You didn't even come after me."

"I am not coming after you. I don't want drama, and I am trying to sleep," I asserted. I couldn't believe this woman. One minute she was making love to me and the next thing she was screaming her brains out. I assumed that since she was an airline stewardess, she would just head to the airport. But boy o' boy, was I wrong. I saw her at the pool the next day. Apparently, she must have spent the night with someone else. I have no idea what happened. She just disappeared on me. To this day, I have no idea what I did. How could a great beginning completely bomb? She would not take my calls, and that was the end of it. Maybe she flew on the next red-eye out. I will never know.

Bruce in Atlanta, Georgia

You and your lady were not on the same page in a relationship. I often hear men complain about making effort only to discover the level of real interest is not mutual. Better communication could have salvaged the expense of heartbreak hotel. Constant complaints, insecurities, lack of appreciation, and the constant need for attention was the flashing neon sign that read, "She's just not that into you, but very into herself!"

FROM EGYPT WITH LOVE

It was the fall of 1996, and I was ready for a change in my life. I started packing up my office and house and putting the boxes into a storage shed I decided to rent. I was interviewing with Procter and Gamble, Genie Garage Door Openers, and Black and Decker. I made it through five interviews and written tests, and it was just a matter of where I was moving. Simultaneously, I was exploring the new world of online dating. I found a few gentlemen to email and had a few more email me. Then, this sexy sultry Egyptian man who was residing in Alabama started emailing me. In November and all through December, we corresponded regularly. By January, I was in love, and that was all there was to it. I had seen all his pictures but would only post my description online. I was tired of men falling in love with their eyes and not their hearts. I wanted him to know who I was.

By February, he was proposing. "Just marry me," he'd say. So finally, by the end of March, I sent him my picture. By then he had proposed 100 times. During April, I agreed to let him fly up to meet me in May if he gave me his SS#, DL#, DOB, and Passport# so I could have a background check done on him. It's nice to have friends in the DA's office! They said other than a few speeding tickets, he was who he said he was, and all seemed well. Rules were he had to stay at a hotel and couldn't know where I lived. He agreed, so we made flight arrangements for him to come into Pittsburgh to see me. We were both so nervous and excited to finally meet. I waited at the gate as the plane pulled in, and the anticipation of him finally walking through that door was really getting to me. It was electric when our eyes first met, and there were the biggest smiles and hearts jumping with joy when we met. We had small chitchat about his flight and workday as we walked hand in hand down the long terminal.

Then when we came to the center rotunda, he stopped, spun me around to face him, dropped his carry-on bag, grabbed my other hand in his, and fell to his knees in front of me. He had the biggest brown eyes, longest eyelashes, and a smile that could melt any heart. There, he continued to repeat over and over, "Tammie, marry me. Please marry me, Tammie. I love you, Tammie. Just marry me, and we will be happy. Tammie, I love you. Marry me. Marry me!" I was so embarrassed and kept pulling on his arms and hands to get up and begging him to please just stop it. By this point, people were starting to circle around us, making me more embarrassed, and he just kept laying it on even thicker and begging me to marry him. I couldn't get him on his feet. The airport police thought there was a fight, so they came over to check out the situation. He yelled, "Officer, officer! Arrest this woman! She has stolen my heart."

At this point, I finally got him to his feet and onto the escalator with every eye in the airport on us. If he didn't have my heart in full before, then he sure did before we got out of that airport. Our weekend was magical with the highlights of Pittsburgh at the restaurants and lookouts on Mt. Washington, the incline rides, and the strip district shopping and foods. That weekend, River Dance was playing at the arena, and I got us tickets. We had a blast. We decided that I should come to Birmingham and stay for a month with him and see how we got along. I had my clients email and send my work there while I continued my interview processes. He said whichever company I went to, he would move with me and find a consulting job there.

We went to Cancun, Cosumel, Opryland, Nashville, Huntsville, and Chattanooga, where we danced all the bronzed dance steps in the sidewalk streets. We talked about getting married, where we'd live, retiring in Egypt, and perhaps adopting or trying various fertility processes since he was told all his life he was sterile by three doctors. Needless to say, by the end of the month, I was pregnant. A few hard weeks of disbelief and realization set in. We were going to be parents. He was not sterile. It was a gift from God. We were going to have a baby. I was already packed and simply had to get a truck and haul it all down to Alabama and arrange for family to move into my house in Pennsylvania.

Life went well. Our son was nine months old, and I stopped breast-feeding him and got pregnant that week with our daughter. I then stopped breast-feeding our daughter when she was six months old and got pregnant that week with our third child. We were visiting with family and friends in Egypt, and I was getting sick and just didn't feel well. On the bus to the airport, I prayed to God that if something was wrong with this baby or there was some reason that I should not have this baby or could not take care of this baby to please take it from me then. Within thirty minutes, I lost our baby. We decided to wait for my body to recover and to try again in six months.

Life was still great. My husband took another two trips to Egypt. Each trip, he took one of the children along with him while I stayed home with the other. Children under two fly free, so there was one last trip for each before their birthdays. We were planning another family trip in October for all of us.

I left for Pennsylvania on September 10, as he was leaving for California on the 13. The day after the World Trade Center was the day my world fell apart. The cell phone call was from my neighbor while I was at a business meeting with investors for my PottieStickers invention on September 12. She informed me that my husband told her to please walk our dog because he had a horrible case of cancer. I was in shock and disbelief. I asked her to repeat herself again. Needless to say, the twenty-minute drive to my mom's house took ten minutes. I had to get to a regular phone. I called, and he hung up on me. I called him again, and he hung up on me. I called the third time and said "Don't hang up. I am renting a car to come home or will be on the first plane out of Pennsylvania if the President lifts the air ban. Regardless, I will be there tomorrow, and we will fight this thing together." We had to get a Will made up and put my name on all the accounts and face the future. He died a few weeks later. I promised him one way or another I would get him home to the family crypt in Cairo, Egypt, to lay beside his father. God knew my limit was two kids. God knew what was in store for me. I had a two-and three-year-old to raise alone. Since my husband did not believe in life insurance, I started marketing my invention, and we donate a percentage to cancer research in his memory. Although our life together wasn't long, I feel lucky that I was able to find my soul mate and fall in love, even if it wasn't long lived.

Tammie in Pittsburg, Pennsylvania

A Remaining Thought

Seizing the whirlwind of "dating technology" has truly been an educational adventure on how to market to the masses for a relationship. We can vouch for the interesting opportunities presented online—from meeting some amazing articulate men, to humorous encounters, to forging wonderful friendships. It transcends limiting ourselves socially as evidenced when we have met charming men online only to discover we had a host of common friends and acquaintances who never got around to introducing us. You just never know the path you might cross in the world of cyber connections. We hope you are enlightened with a glimpse of the real deal in online dating. We wish you much success if you decide to join the crowd to find love. We encourage you to have fun along the way, laugh occasionally… and oh… while you are shopping online be sure to keep yourself entertained!

We would love for you to share your online stories or dating experiences!

Login to www.LoveSexand Deception.com for a free bonus on the website. We feature a Q & A Forum on dating advice and related articles. Receive our monthly e-newsletter featuring submitted stories and questions. including our advice column.

ABOUT THE AUTHORS

CLAIRE HULTIN has recently published her first book entitled: The Doctrine Of Lucid Dreaming and is also the founder of www.dreaminglucidly.com. She specializes in topics such as psychology, oneirology, (the study of dreams) and international business. Claire is also the owner of an LLC called Electronic Novelties © which is a business that specifically deals with the import/export of electronics and Scandinavian products. She occasionally dabbles in graffiti/comic art projects, and works with a modeling agency known as Runi Rone photography and well-known photography by Udara Soysa. She has also recently invented Multi-Microchip Clocks © and is currently working on a highly innovative program that is related to memory retention and extensive learning. Her personalized website www.clairehultin.com elaborates more in depth on her projects.

Claire is also a strong social-political activist and humanitarian but is currently focusing on transformational activism. She strives to volunteer her time and effort with the SIA Orphan Association, AOA-Asian Orphan's Association, and the non profit organization called, SCE-Stop Child Executions, which is an organization that raises awareness and aims to put an end to child executions in Iran.

Claire also assisted with non-profit organizations that are relevant to the explosive and shocking genocide in Darfur. Such organizations are STAND: A Student Anti-Genocide Coalition, UNHCR, The Genocide Intervention Network, and the Save Darfur Coalition.

LISA HULTIN graduated with a Bachelor of Arts degree in telecommunications from Liberty University, Lynchburg, Virginia. She started off her political career working as an intern in the U.S. House of Representatives for Congressman Wayne Dowdy from McComb, Mississippi. Lisa Hultin then married and lived overseas in the city of Goteborg, Sweden. After relocating to Atlanta, GA she worked on the production for the TV pilot "The Profiler" which later became a renowned television series.

A woman of many entrepreneurial skills, she became the owner of Maywood O.P. and the MM company, which is a commercial real-estate property in Jackson, Mississippi. Furthermore, she started her own Scandinavian import/export business in which she exported Scandinavian fireplaces made from the finest decorative tiles.

Lisa was also a major fundraiser for Atlanta charities and cultural organizations such as The Atlanta Opera and March Of Dimes. She also hosted the Alliance Theatre Christmas House.

Lisa is also the writer of the blog for www. LoveSexandDeception.com and resides in Atlanta, Georgia.

BUY A SHARE OF THE FUTURE IN YOUR COMMUNITY

These certificates make great holiday, graduation and birthday gifts that can be personalized with the recipient's name. The cost of one S.H.A.R.E. or one square foot is $54.17. The personalized certificate is suitable for framing and will state the number of shares purchased and the amount of each share, as well as the recipient's name. The home that you participate in "building" will last for many years and will continue to grow in value.

Here is a sample SHARE certificate:

HABITAT FOR HUMANITY

THIS CERTIFIES THAT

YOUR NAME HERE

HAS INVESTED IN A HOME FOR A DESERVING FAMILY

1985-2005

TWENTY YEARS OF BUILDING FUTURES IN OUR
COMMUNITY ONE HOME AT A TIME

1200 SQUARE FOOT HOUSE @ $65,000 = $54.17 PER SQUARE FOOT
This certificate represents a tax deductible donation. It has no cash value.

YES, I WOULD LIKE TO HELP!

I support the work that Habitat for Humanity does and I want to be part of the excitement! As a donor, I will receive periodic updates on your construction activities but, more importantly, I know my gift will help a family in our community realize the dream of homeownership. **I would like to SHARE in your efforts against substandard housing in my community!** *(Please print below)*

PLEASE SEND ME _____ SHARES at $54.17 EACH = $ $_____

In Honor Of: _____

Occasion: (Circle One)   HOLIDAY   BIRTHDAY   ANNIVERSARY

      OTHER: _____

Address of Recipient: _____

Gift From: _____ *Donor Address:* _____

Donor Email: _____

I AM ENCLOSING A CHECK FOR $ $_____ PAYABLE TO HABITAT FOR HUMANITY OR PLEASE CHARGE MY VISA OR MASTERCARD *(CIRCLE ONE)*

Card Number _____ Expiration Date: _____

Name as it appears on Credit Card _____ Charge Amount $ _____

Signature _____

Billing Address _____

Telephone # Day _____ Eve _____

PLEASE NOTE: Your contribution is tax-deductible to the fullest extent allowed by law.
Habitat for Humanity • P.O. Box 1443 • Newport News, VA 23601 • 757-596-5553
www.HelpHabitatforHumanity.org

Printed in the USA
CPSIA information can be obtained
at www.ICGtesting.com
JSHW082203140824
68134JS00014B/398